All rights reserved. No part of this book may be reproduced in any form or by any electronic or mechanical means, without the expressed consent from the publisher, except brief passages for reviewers.

Capitol Press Publishing
New York , New York
Visit our website at
www.CapitolPressPublishing.com

Copyright © 2017 by Adam Taft Lambert

First Capitol Press trade paperback edition November 2017
Reissue November 2023

For information about special discounts for bulk purchases, please contact Capitol Press Publishing.

The Capitol Press Speakers Bureau can bring authors to your live event. For information and to set up a booking, contact the Capitol Press Speakers Bureau
CapitolPressPublishing@gmail.com

Third Edition

Manufactured in the United States
of America

3 5 7 9 8 6 4

ISBN (TP): 9780999499009

HIGHLIGHTS FROM THE FIRST

ADAM TAFT LAMBERT

ESSAYS

WHAT'S IN A NAME?	11
WAKEY, WAKEY, EGGS & BAKEY	23
CONVERSATIONS WITH MY BROTHER #1	33
THE NIGHT BUS TO LOUISVILLE	35
TUESDAYS IN LEXINGTON	59
GOOD WINTER, PART I	73
AN HONORABLE DEATH	83
CONVERSATIONS WITH MY BROTHER #2	95
SCENES IN THE STREET	97
NOTES ON A CORNER STORE	105
GOOD WINTER, PART II	121
THE HORCRUX OF THE PLAN	131
CONVERSATIONS WITH MY BROTHER #3	151

ACKNOWLEDGEMENTS

**FOR MA
&
POPS**

**A VERY SPECIAL THANKS TO MY EDITOR,
LINDSEY AMICK**

HIGHLIGHTS FROM THE FIRST

WHAT'S IN A NAME?

I remember the date—May 20th, 2009. That's the date that Paula Abdul, Randy Jackson, Simon Cowell, some woman named Kara, and the 100 million Americans who voted during season eight of *American Idol* tuned in to find out who would be crowned the winner. It's the date that I, and what felt like the rest of the world, sat back in stunned amazement when contestant, Kris Allen, was crowned champion over the fan-favorite Adam Lambert.

Despite the immediate obviousness of why I was so invested, it's important to lay it out for clarity's sake. The runner-up and I both have the same first name. Adam. It's a common name and probably not enough to draw you into a season of *American Idol*. But there's more. We both have the same last name, Lambert. Lambert is less common than Adam, but it's still a fairly recognizable last name around the world. I'll spare you the etymological details, but suffice it to say Lambert is common enough throughout many European languages, it allows me to dance in and out of multiple ethnic identities as the need arises (Lambrecht for German, Lamberti in Italian, Lamb*ert* in French, etc.). So, first name and last name, those are the obvious parts. There's still more.

We were also both raised in the Midwest. And, as everyone from the Midwest will readily explain to you, that makes us a slightly different class of people. Mostly, that means we both likely harbor a seething hostility just beneath our well-meaning Midwestern appearance. But it also just about guarantees that his parents also struggled with properly portioning meals to their children—a classic Midwestern trait. Another similarity between us: we are both A.C.O.D. (IYKYK)

Adam and I were both born in the 1980s. He in '82, and me '88. True, that's grasping-at-straws in terms of similarities, but I'm counting it. A more specific similarity is that we were both born in late January. If you are a practitioner of the astrological arts, you'll know that makes both him and me Aquarians, which—in addition to being both frank and imaginative—also means we're both unpredictable and detached. I'm going to count that one, too.

Aside from the name and all the other details, there is one final connection between us, one that I'm building up to. One that people in the poker world might call a *kicker*. And the kicker is this: Adam Lambert and I were both born on the same day, January 29th.

To quickly recap the identification triumvirate, Adam Lambert and I have the same *first* name, same *last* name, and the same birthday. If it doesn't seem like much now, you'll be forgiven for not grasping the full weight of the information I've presented to you. It is much more than just some quirky administrative details at play here.

Now, I don't know if *I* would consider Adam Lambert an A-list celebrity, but B-list? We can all agree on that. And I get that beginning your journey to stardom on a reality show usually shackles someone to being C-list certified their whole life, but he's successfully graduated to the next level. And while that was good for him, it wasn't always so great for me.

In the beginning, during the actual season of *American Idol*, when The Other Adam Lambert's (TOAL) appeal began to grow, there were only a few passing comments from people I knew, none of which I understood. I would randomly receive texts from friends asking what store was best for "guyliner" or "man-gernail polish." The nickname "Glambert" would be floated around now and again, but I mostly just ignored it. I chose instead to remain in my default setting of turning a blind eye to whatever was happening around me and hoping that somehow it would just, like, you know, go away or something.

Looking back now, thinking that way was idiotic. With all of the coverage and publicity TOAL garnered during his months-long run on *American Idol*, the fact that I could remain so ignorant of a presence that would soon cause irreversible changes in my life still amazes me. But that ignorance didn't last long. It was shattered by a notorious *Entertainment Weekly* cover on May 15th, 2009.

That edition featured TOAL on the cover, smiling bashfully behind the title, "LOVING ADAM LAMBERT: The Most Exciting '*American Idol*' Contestant in Years*." It was a fairly innocuous headline aside from the asterisk, but that asterisk made all the difference. As your eyes glanced down to the bottom of the page where the asterisk led, you found your additional text:

"*And Not Just Because He Might Be Gay."

Now, there's a lot to unpack here. Culturally, socially, and economically, there are a lot of ways to carve up that line of text; none of them are very good. For starters, *might* be gay? As in, they're still determining, but are just going to throw that out there, ayway? Even in 2009, that seems like a grossly negligent thing to print on the cover of your magazine. To publicly quasi-out someone, even if it is *Entertainment Weekly*, feels irresponsible at best. Still, they must have been happy with their decision because that cover was everywhere.

There's a part of me that feels like my tolerance level and the sales of that magazine were inversely correlated; the more the sales went up, the less I could tolerate. That cover found its way to me through virtually every form of communication imaginable: mail, email, text, social media, all of it. Even hand-delivered, in one instance. I faintly remember my Memaw mentioning that magazine cover to me and the realization that it affected three generations of my family felt like a biblical curse had been placed upon me. Seemingly, every person I knew and every stranger who discovered TOAL and I's shared connection hit me with a wink, an elbow nudge, or any other sort of tongue-in-cheek innuendo for weeks after it was published. The fever eventually died, but the magazine cover, the show, and all our similarities bound us together. And once that happened, our web of attachment expanded in a lot of unexpected ways.

For instance, the television show *Lizzie McGuire* connects me and TOAL. For anyone who is not a millennial, *Lizzie McGuire* was a Disney Channel behemoth in the early aughts that turned its star actor, Hilary Duff, into a household name for the better part of a decade. Content-wise, I'm sure the show was fine. I didn't watch it when I was younger because I was deep in the powerhouse lineup Toonami had put together over on Cartoon Network with *Sailor Moon*, *Dragon Ball Z*, and *Gundam Wing*. Still, the show managed to reach me because *Lizzie McGuire* featured the affable and loveable character named David "Gordo" Gordon, played by a young, upshot actor named Adam Lamberg. Obviously, it's not the same name as me and TOAL (and he was born in September anyway), but that one-letter difference was close enough for my peers to tease me about the association. I can't remember how many times classmates asked me if I liked being an actor on a show their little sisters watched. I'm not sure if TOAL had the same experience, being that he's a few years older, but for me, that connection was a source of a good bit of taunting on the rough-and-tumble blacktops of Gregory Middle School.

And surely I wasn't the only Adam Lambert in America who was milking the Miranda Lambert fame in early 2005, right? I'd tell just about anyone within earshot that she and I were related because that's what you do when you share the last name with a celebrity. Pitt, DiCaprio, Twain (both Mark and Shania), of course, you're going to make that joke—no chance there's a Witherspoon out that hasn't tried to milk the Reese fame. You have to use those kinds of relationships when they present themselves. My brother sure did.

He'd call me up whenever he was out at the bars and needed a good pickup line. I can't blame him. It's unique telling someone your brother is Adam Lambert. And after a while, any call that came in from his number after 11:30 p.m. was formulaic. "Ohmigod, shut up. You're not Adam Lambert. Like the *real* one? Sing something for me! NOW!" I would diffuse the situation by saying I was just getting over a cold—"*The weather is so strange out here in Berlin. I'm on tour.*"—or by passing off some other lame excuse. After that, they'd usually become immediately uninterested. I'd get a quick "Ugh, whatever," and then an abrupt hang-up. It's not the coolest thing I've ever done for my brother, but I like to think it helped him snag a few dates. And while it's nice to put my connection to TOAL to good use, my brother's pickup line, like my Miranda call out, only works because of the shared *last* name of a celebrity. If both names match, it doesn't work. If I went around saying I'm related to Adam Lambert, people would think I'd lost my mind. Existentially, it's a brain-melter, but even if they thought I meant TOAL when I said it, no one is going to believe there are two Adam Lamberts in the same family. That'd be ridiculous. And it's an important difference. There are things you can do when you share a last name with a celebrity that you can't do when you share a full name. It's subtle, but it's important.

I'll mention here that there are positives to having the same name (and birthday) as a relatively famous celebrity. It's created easy, built-in small talk with authority figures and service workers practically since TOAL became famous. It's made going to the DMV a pretty enjoyable experience for me. I usually get a side-eye or two and a pithy comment, but they almost always precede a smile and pleasant conversation. With the TSA, the same thing happens two out of every ten times I travel. Also, you'd be amazed at how many dental hygienists (male and female) know who TOAL is. It gets brought up all the time.

And, yeah, using my name to form an immediate

connection with a stranger is nice, but it can be dangerous in the wrong hands. When I was in college, there was a bar that I would often frequent, a typical college town dive bar serving the local gentry of bartenders and other restaurant workers around the city. It was semi-famous for the crowd that would rally in the late hours of the morning after everywhere else had closed for the night. My best friend is the younger brother of one of the ownership partners there and after our bar shifts elsewhere, we'd make our way down there to decompress. Every so often, when I entered the establishment (and depending on how intoxicated my friend's brother was), this particular owner would quiet the bar and then, in a voice loud enough for all to hear, ask me: "Whaddaya want to drink?," a clever play on Adam Lambert's debut single, "What Do You Want from Me?" He'd cackle and run around the bar, showing everyone pictures of Adam Lambert's notorious debut album cover and announcing to any woman within earshot, "Yeah, they have the same name and birthday. This one's probably gay, too!" Honestly, it's a good bit. It's relevant and only slightly humiliating, like a good joke should be. So, you know, well played to him.

It's similar to the same low-grade embarrassment I'd feel when I'd wake up to find I had a bunch of new followers on social media. Thinking it was because of one of my hilarious tweets, I felt real proud of myself until I saw it was all accounts with names like Glambert4Evr or Glamfan129 or Guyliner10000000000. Ironically, during those brief moments of humiliation, the lyrics to TOAL's "What Do You Want from Me?" provided a fair amount of comfort.

> *"Just don't give up, I am workin' it out*
> *Please don't give in; I won't let you down*
> *It messed me up; need a second to breathe*
> *Just keep coming around…*
> *Hey, whataya want from me?"*

I have tried to contact TOAL several times throughout the years with a random tag in a tweet here and there or a post about each of us on our birthday, but he has never responded. It's understandable to a certain degree. He's a famous musician who gets inundated with hundreds if not thousands of messages, tweets, and tags from people all over the planet every day; people who—let's admit it—are probably seeking more genuine contact with the man than I am. I don't know why I reached out, to be honest, because I don't know what I would do if he responded. It would be cool to be featured in *People Magazine* or on *Buzzfeed* in one of those "These Normals Have the Same Names as Celebs!" sections. It's great clickbait. But anything more than that, and I start getting bothered by the whole idea. It starts to feel weird pretty quickly, which is probably why I stopped trying to contact him.

For so long, I've dealt with people comparing me to

TOAL and making jokes. And, yeah, I get it. They are jokes. I'm not really asking for that to go away. But most people can't grasp how existentially paralyzing it is to be stripped of your identity, even in the seemingly petty inconvenience of sharing a name (and a birthday) with a celebrity. Your name and your birthday are two of the most individual characteristics of one's life. Having them separated from their inherent descriptions and having someone else's life invade your own without having any say in the matter is a horrible feeling. It's the kind of drama that people write plays about. Arthur Miller did it in *The Crucible*. Victor Hugo wrote a thousand-plus-page novel about it in *Les Mis*. I wish I had this experience while reading those works in high school. I get it now—*Because it is my name!*—it hits so hard. Think about every job application, restaurant reservation, and doctor's visit; any time you interact or communicate with someone new for the first time, your name takes on a new meaning if it's always met with a sly grin or you constantly hear someone giggling about it on the other side of the phone.

And for all our similarities, TOAL doesn't get that part of it. He doesn't—*he can't*—understand it. This situation can never be reversed. TOAL can never feel the same way I do. You are either the namesake or the comparison. You are the famous one, or you are the normal one. And celebrities cannot become *un*famous. TOAL will never *not* be known as the world-famous musician Adam Lambert. His star may fade, he may cease to be relevant, or even become *in*famous for something later on, but he will always be the famous one. He will always be *the* Adam Lambert.

I've asked myself a lot of questions over the years about this situation: is it funny? Should I laugh along with it? Should I make another Michael Bolton *Office Space* reference? Should I get angry? Should I even care? Over and over again, with every wink, every laugh, every surprised expression at hearing my name, TOAL's words echo in my head, *what do you want from me?*

And in all the years, I never found a satisfying answer for how to deal with it, but it's because I've been asking the wrong question. I've been missing something. It's something different. The question I should really be asking is…what do *I* want from me?

WAKEY, WAKEY, EGGS & BAKEY

I am thoroughly convinced that people who wake up in the morning and make themselves breakfast are, for the most part, assholes. I have heard the evidence to the contrary. "Breakfast is the most important meal of the day." "It helps get your day started." "Ron Swanson, man. Eggs and Bacon. *All* the eggs and bacon. Didn't you watch *Parks & Rec?*" And I still don't get why people are so jazzed about breakfast.

For one, sleeping is, without a doubt, the greatest part of the human experience. Arguably one of the most important, as well. Anyone who tells you otherwise probably wakes up early to make themselves breakfast (see earlier comment). I'm not talking about the overindulgence of sleeping or the "adulting-is-hard" I'm-staying-in-bed type of sleep. I am talking about the true-blue Americana type of sleeping. The laying down after a long day's work or a hard night of drinking. The type of sleep you get any time you put real gumption into something and then, unencumbered by distractions or disturbances, sleep like a stone, is the closest we will ever get to heaven on this earthly realm. Those who have the opportunity to take part in that sacrament and choose to forgo its full measure are disturbed at best and are, at the very least, well…I think you get it.

What's the point, anyway, if you have to make breakfast yourself? Nothing tastes better than something given to and/or made for you. So, attempting to wake up early and create a culinary experience of value for yourself is ridiculous. If someone else wants to wake up early and make you breakfast, then by all means, encourage them. Smile tenderly, be generous with gratitude, and accept whatever it is they are offering to you politely. Even if it's crap food, it is better than having to wake up to make that crap food yourself and then feed that crap into your crap mouth, right? So, if you intend to be the kind of person who wakes up to make themselves breakfast, my suggestion to you is to reevaluate your priorities. Hit the snooze button, pull up the covers, and sleep a little longer.

Now, before this goes any further, it's important to note that I understand how this opinion may make me appear: a man exhausting himself about how stupid it is to wake up early, arguing that people doing things for him is a better way to live…I get it. It's very immature. Honestly, it's worse than that. It's childish. Fetal is probably an even better description.

And I accept those possible perceptions. I accept them because, though my opinion may be juvenile, it was an opinion that I came to through an honest attempt at the alternative.

A few weeks ago, believing that being an early riser was the sign of being a mature adult, I decided that was what I wanted to do for the rest of my life. Never let the sun catch you in bed sort of stuff. I knew it would be difficult, but I had tackled difficult tasks before, and this time, I was determined to see it through. To create a new life and make myself into a new man. A man who wakes up early.

But things went south quickly. I was not prepared. Even with the new event jitters and excitement that usually push you through discomfort, I wasn't ready for the anger that met me for having to leave my bed even half a second earlier than the last possible moment. It was that seething, irrational anger that flares up behind the wheel when someone cuts you off or any time you're standing in a line of strangers—that feral beast type of anger. Generally, you can offset some of the frustration by blaming someone else, "Pick a lane, dumbass!!" or "What are these people doing here? Can't you shop for groceries any other time besides the exact time I have to?" But this time, I didn't have the option to offload because I was the reason. All of that anger was directed at myself. Which, actually, is pretty standard.

Luckily, I assumed the beast would wake with me in the morning, so I concocted a plan. The night before, I strategically placed my phone (alarm) in another part of the apartment. I have read lots of places online that it is imperative to put it in another room if you want to wake up early. Actually, anyone who's anyone about providing productivity tips and life hacks will readily explain to you that doing this is absolutely essential for sleeping undisturbed and waking up earlier. It's pretty much the top mental health hack that shows up when you search for something along the lines of how to make my life better—put your phone in another room. Unfortunately, we live in a studio apartment, and as such, "another room" is hard to come by. For my part, though, I did choose the space our apartment listing generously described as "the kitchen" for the "another room" to put my phone in and went to bed believing I was in good hands because on paper, this idea makes sense. But the big grift about this hack, though, the thing nobody on YouTube or Instagram has cared to explain is what you are supposed to do when the Jekyll-adjacent fury-monster shows up at 6:05 a.m. mad as hell, looking to fight, and all you're equipped with is a stupid "no phones in the bedroom" rule to defend yourself.

I'll spare you the details of the epic fight between me and the beast that happened over the nine steps it takes for me to get from my bed to my kitchen. That's a story for another time. Once I was in the kitchen, I knew there was only one thing that could help me. My girlfriend Erin and I had recently decided to switch to instant espresso, and because it was mostly my decision to switch, I think it's amazing. You take a cup, add some powder, a little boiling water, and boom, you have a cup of energy for your morning. But don't try to church it up; just get Café Bustelo. It's the cheapest and the best. Instant espresso is also great because it completely erases the most frustrating part of the morning coffee-making process: the excess coffee that you always make and then never use. That little bit of coffee that sits in the pitcher, laughing at you, knowing how angry it will make you when you first have to dump out the old sludge and wash out the entrails the next morning before you make the new coffee. I hated that part. Thus, instant espresso.

Anyway, I crossed the threshold to the kitchen, silenced the blaring alarm on my phone, and went through my instant espresso powder protocol. Then, with a belly full of Bustelo, I set out to make myself ~~into an asshole~~ breakfast.

On the menu that morning was only one item—an egg sandwich. Like any good New Yorker, I am a huge fan of the-egg-plus-meat-plus-cheese-on-bagel-style-sandwiches. Most prefer the iconic B.E.C. (bacon, egg, and cheese), but I'm more of a sausage guy (no regrets). It was that love of the egg-plus-meat-plus-cheese-on-bagel-style-sandwich that inspired this whole morning revolution in the first place. A few days prior, I bought an egg sandwich from the street vendor at the end of my block on my way to work. After succumbing to the usual delight of eating something that was given and/or made for you, it dawned on me that I could do this myself. I was soaring pretty high on a D.I.Y. kick on account of being broke, which included tailoring my own clothes and scavenging all my furniture so it made a lot of sense to add Chef to the list of professional titles I was taking on. And there I was a few days later with high hopes, middling anger, and a can-do spirit, standing in my kitchen with two eggs, three pieces of turkey bacon, one slice of cheddar cheese, and a hamburger bun as a substitute bagel in front of me, trying real hard to slap nature in the face.

Okay. First things first: bacon in the skillet. Since it was turkey bacon, the preparation is a bit different than your normal run-of-the-mill pork bacon. Directions: Cook in a skillet over medium-high heat. Flip *constantly*. Never break eye contact with your turkey bacon. Never forget that this is not real bacon. (If you're in a rush—or if you wish to further the point that you have given up on life—you may cook your turkey bacon in the microwave.) There I stood, counting to 14 in my head and then flipping the three perfectly processed ugly pink and gray strips over and over and over and over again for eight to ten minutes. The time commitment for cooking turkey bacon is grueling, but it does leave one with just the right amount of time to wax poetic about a topic or theme.

There is something intrinsically nostalgic about breakfast. It reminds me of childhood, of carefree moments, free of responsibility and decision. A good time, a better time.

It was a time when people were always giving and/or making things for you. With breakfast, specifically the cooking of bacon, I always think of my mother. The crackling of bacon in the skillet reminds me of her rally cry to get me and my siblings out of bed and come downstairs: "Wakey, Wakey, Eggs & Bakey!" I have such vivid memories of her exalting her declaration standing guard over the stove top, draped in an oversized t-shirt, while she slapped away bacon grease with a bare hand. It was memories like that one I had hoped would be triggered when I got up that morning to make breakfast. Unfortunately, because of my mother's southern heritage—and because she cares about us deeply—she never subjected my siblings and me to turkey bacon; therefore, those fond memories never materialized. Instead, as I looked down at the raw strips in the pan, rather than being dropped into a childhood reverie or filled with the warm embrace of thoughts of my mother, all I could see were three gross-looking rubber bands whose edges were dancing awkwardly on top of the crackling fat they were secreting into the pan. It was a defeating feeling. And it certainly wasn't the only time I would feel it throughout the morning, but at least the bacon was cooked.

With the bacon done and set aside, I could move on to cooking the eggs. I added some olive oil to the pan, let it heat a bit, then popped the buns into the pan to toast. This part turned out well despite the slightly charred buns and the oil burns on my knuckles. I needed the win because the next part of the process was by far the worst.

If you have ever tried to cook eggs with an ill-measured amount of lubricant, then you know the eggs you are trying to cook will turn out terribly. Hence the phrase I made up: "Hell hath no fury like a person who has fucked up fried eggs." The problem, of course, is poor decision-making. Either you have added too much or not added enough. In my case, it was too little, and this Mama Bear scenario got out of hand quickly. And by the time you notice these eggs are not doing what they are supposed to be doing, it's too late. You can't think about your poor decision-making skills. You can't think of any rational thought, for that matter, because you are too busy scraping and negotiating a rubber spatula around a pan thats heat setting, somehow, got way too high for what you are trying to cook. The only thing you can focus on is how to get as many scraps of eggs out of the pan in one piece. I tried to fight it off, but the Morning Monster returned and took complete control of my nervous system, beginning an internal monologue that featured some real vile and awful things about my qualities as a person.

As the cerebral onslaught continued, beads of sweat began forming and then streaked wildly down the sides of my face like some sort of horrible sled hill from hell. The clothes I was wearing began to constrict around me as they first became water-logged with sweat and then suctioned by the heat of the stovetop. The longer I kept up my fight against the eggs, the worse it got. I knew I couldn't defeat an enemy of this magnitude. It was too powerful. I yielded. I cut off the heat, scraped the roadkill remnants out of the pan, and formed what remained into a pile on top of the burnt bun. I was so mad at this point I practically punched the fucking turkey bacon onto the top. But the real coup de grâce was the slice of cheddar I wanted to use for the sandwich. It had been sitting out on the counter the whole time I was preparing the rest of the meal and was now drenched in more sweat than I was. It, too, joined the putrid pile of filth I had produced for breakfast. I wiped my face and checked the clock—6:43 a.m.

At this point, I think it is important to note that Erin, a preternaturally heavy sleeper, almost always awakens to the sounds and smells of bacon cooking, turkey or otherwise. This time was no exception. But her waking up was a part of the morning I hadn't accounted for. Maybe it was because I was in the midst of a rage stroke from cooking the eggs; maybe it was because I knew she would soon be back to sleep; maybe it was because I am a selfish piece of trash. Whatever the reason, I didn't make her a breakfast sandwich which, as she pointed out later, "was disappointing" and, as I pointed out earlier, makes me an asshole.

To be fair, once I was away from the scene of the crime and able to view it with a little more clarity, the sandwich looked fine and tasted okay. It would have made for a pretty nice breakfast if it had been given to and/or made for me.

Perhaps while still in bed, with a glass of cold orange juice and some coffee. But, since that was not the situation, the whole vibe around the sandwich was, in a word, upsetting.

As I had predicted, Erin soon fell back asleep. I took my sandwich, what was left of my second cup of espresso (what, you think I stopped at just one?), and a napkin out onto our terrace. To clarify, our terrace is what we call the broken chair next to the window of our garbage-facing, garden-view studio apartment. There I sat, the dregs of my second cup beside me, a somewhat edible egg and turkey bacon sandwich on a hamburger bun in my lap, and a mostly blocked view of Upper West Siders' ankles in front of me. I was filled with the underwhelming pride of starting my day off right.

When I finished eating and cleaning, it was time to shower and get ready for work. The whole time, though, instead of feeling accomplished or productive like I was lied into believing I would by social media, I felt quite different. I felt strange. I felt as though someone kept poking an index finger into my abdomen. Not dangerous, but consistent and annoying. Like toddlers. It was the kind of discomfort you don't care much about, but you can't simply ignore it; it will only worsen. That pain followed me out the door, down into the subway, across the platform to my transfer, and finally into my building, where, at my desk, instead of being the productive, energetic member of society I believed I would become after making myself breakfast, I thought long and hard about how I could take the rest of the day off.

Eventually, I pulled the trigger and left. Told the employer I was too sick to work and needed to go home. I'm not proud of it. I knew it was the wrong thing to do. I did it anyway. But, honestly, what did you expect? I'm the type of person who wakes up and makes myself breakfast.

CONVERSATIONS WITH MY BROTHER #1

Howie Day's "Collide" is playing over the loudspeaker at Target.

My brother (to me): "Your phone's ringing."

THE NIGHT BUS TO LOUISVILLE

The night bus from New York City to Louisville, Kentucky, leaves from 59 Canal Street in the Chinatown neighborhood of Manhattan at 11:23 p.m. and lasts for 13 hours. I know this because I took this bus in November 2015 with Erin to get to Louisville for Thanksgiving. This is that story.

Before anyone formulates any opinions of their own, let me explain a few things about riding a cross-country bus from the get-go. The only reason anyone travels by cross-country bus is because they can't afford the alternative. There are no two ways around that. There is no scenic reason for traveling across the country on a bus (especially not on an overnight bus); there is no nostalgia factor at play here—if there was ever a bygone era of bus traveling in this country, it's certainly not catered to now. Traveling by bus is an economic decision made, most likely, under pretty dire circumstances. And while, yes, you are generally saving money traveling by bus, there *is* a cost to your penny-pinching.

I had never done extended traveling by bus before this trip. For those who haven't either, here's a quick Q&A to help answer some of the important questions about traveling in this capacity.

Q: Is 13 hours on a bus as bad as it sounds?

A: It is.

Q: Are the seats on a 13-hour bus ride as uncomfortable as you imagine?

A: They are.

Q: Do the odors emanating and coalescing from 49 different strangers over 13 hours on a bus create as noxious a smell as you think it might?

A: Of course.

Q: Are there people who would dare eat cottage cheese from a Tupperware container on a crowded, overnight, 13-hour bus ride?

A: Absolutely there are. This is America.

And finally, if you're wondering how one person could withstand such horrid conditions and still retain enough mental faculties to captain a bus around the highways and byways of America without threat to the life or limb of those on board, don't worry; they don't. But more on that later. There's still a lot to tell about traveling by bus.

Every time I tell people I have taken a Chinatown bus as

a form of transportation, a few things generally happen. First, there comes that soft, pitying smile that appears whenever someone realizes they are speaking to a person from a lower rung of the socio-economic ladder. They hear the word "bus," their eyes glaze over, and the corners of their mouth bend slightly upward, and they start figuring out how to get out of the conversation. You know they're thinking it, they know you know they're thinking, but everyone just keeps smiling and nodding like we're not in the worst possible conversation on the entire planet. The next thing that happens depends on how long that person can endure proximity to an Untouchable. If they don't exit the conversation immediately, they will impart a compassionate gaze and then ask—in a tone I'm not super fond of—if traveling by bus cross-country is worth it. What happens next is a tricky bit of interpersonal communication because that's not really the question they are asking me, and that's not really the question I end up answering. What they are *really* asking me is if I am proud of the choices that I have made in my life; if I am—as my mother used to ask her misbehaving first-grade students—"proud of the decisions I am making." The question that I am answering is whether subjecting myself to that kind of torture and humiliation will be enough for me to change my ways and finally live a better life. The answer for both is, I don't know. Probably not.

But I do know that once you've borne the hardship of something like traveling 13 hours on a bus, once you've entered into the social contract that constitutes an overnight bus trip and have your humanity stripped and your reality shattered by such an endeavor, you will undeniably emerge on the other side a changed person.

Our transformation began, as the most intense transformations often do, in a foreign environment. We were in Chinatown, which is located in Lower Manhattan, with borders alongside Little Italy, TriBeCa, and the Lower East Side. It is a curious and enthralling place. Chinatown sober is a lot like everywhere else drunk, especially after dark. The immediate adjectives that jump to mind are loud, chaotic, disorienting, exciting, frightening, shameful, claustrophobic, and aggressive. With a perpetual coating of hazy cigarette smoke hanging right around the head level, it is exceedingly difficult to catch your bearings as you careen between fish stands, strangers hawking knock-off purses, and claw machines that are inexplicably filled with assorted watches and cell phones of indiscriminate origin. At night, the harsh and ever-present neon signs begin to affect your vision the more you adventure. Garbage and creatures crunch and reel beneath your feet as you stumble along the uneven pavement. Your mind begins to unravel as you search for some obscure, vaguely remembered address; *"Bowery and Broome, right? Yo, is that a rat or a raccoon!? No, wait, it was by the Bowery. Off Grand Street? But, wait, this says Chrystie Street—dude, it was a rat! It was huge. Why the hell is that park named after Columbus? Why are there so many rats?!"* All the while, the ubiquitous smell of fish seeps into everything and everyone.

For an outsider, Chinatown isn't so much unsafe as it is uncertain. Or rather you, as the outsider, are uncertain. There are no points of reference there. There are no familiar sites, no context clues from which you could gain a foothold of understanding. If you're like me, nothing from your lily-white upbringing in Midwest America can prepare you to be so out of touch with an environment. Everything is different, and everything is strange. Much like the rest of Manhattan, it's not unwelcoming; it's indifferent. In Chinatown, you will either be stared at by a stranger for an amount of time that should be illegal or are so wholly and completely ignored as to feel inescapably irrelevant. It produces an isolation that no other part of New York, perhaps the world, is capable of competing with. All the while, your mind is in constant conflict over whether where you are is where you are supposed to be. It just doesn't ever connect.

At this point, it's fair to make the assumption there is no way an overnight bus ride out of a place like Chinatown is safe, right? And the truth is, no, it's not really that safe. In 2006, New York Senator Chuck Schumer demanded the Department of Transportation get tougher on the Chinatown buses after a devastating report on their safety. The report revealed that Greyhound Buses, which routinely receive a zero on the safety scale (zero being the best on a 0-100 scale),

Chinatown buses, on average, score between 71 and 99. Yeah, not great. Adding to that, there was a whole string of rather alarming and particularly gruesome attacks between 2003 and 2004 that all centered around Chinatown buses. I could summarize, but the description from Wikipedia conveying the severity of the situation should really be read in full:

> "The bus lines have drawn scrutiny from law enforcement authorities for possible connections to Chinese organized crime gangs. In 2003 and 2004, a number of bus arsons, driver assaults, murders, and other gang violence in New York City were linked to the possible infiltration of Asian organized crime gangs into the industry.
>
> Among the crimes believed to have been associated with gang activity was a deadly shooting in May 2003, on a busy street, which may have been in retaliation for a driver having backed his bus into a rival; as revenge, two buses were set on fire in 2004. There was a fatal stabbing in October 2003, as well as another unrelated stabbing in 2004. In January 2004, the boyfriend of a bus worker was lethally shot in what appeared to be a bus feud, and in March 2004, a Chinatown bus operator was killed in yet another fatal shooting. In a June 2004 incident tied to criminal gangs, two people—a Chinatown bus

driver and a bystander—were murdered in a bar in Flushing, Queens, and another was shot in the leg. The accused shooter was arrested in Toronto in 2011 and extradited to the United States. After the 2004 shootings, the New York City Police Department (NYPD) started enforcing Chinatown bus rules more strictly."

So, safety-wise, it's a real shot in the dark. But safety is only one of many hurdles you have to overcome once you decide to take a bus out of Chinatown. The next big decision you have to make is *which* bus you are going to take because—as I have yet to mention—you cannot take *the* Chinatown bus; you take *a* Chinatown bus. Which one depends on your final destination. For instance, if you want to go to Boston, you could take the Fung Wah bus or the Lucky Star. If you're headed to D.C., you could take the Eastern or Dragon bus. Baltimore? You're going to be on the Double Happiness bus. Cleveland? You're taking the Fook Sing. The more time you spend in Chinatown, the more you notice signs that are all variations on the theme: a white background with blue or red lettering—only a few of which are in English—showing things like NYC—> DC—> VA. or NYC—> CT—> BOS. Those are the embarkation points for these landside cruises. They point you in the right direction.

Our bus for the trip to Louisville turned out to be the

Jaguar bus. Not the Panda or Panther as we'd hoped, but a noble animal nonetheless. The Jaguar bus, unlike a lot of the others, makes no East Coast stops. It bounds out of New York, hellbent on the Midwest, and doesn't stop till it reaches Columbus, Ohio. After that, it stops twice in Cincinnati, Ohio and then finally comes to rest in Louisville, Kentucky. The reasons why it stops twice in Cincinnati are unclear. The time of our departure, according to the ticket, was 10:30 p.m. Since we'd never traveled this way before, Erin and I decided it might be wise for us to arrive a few hours early. The assumption being that bus departures, surely, would operate in a similar capacity to something like Southwest Airlines. In other words, the earlier you check in and get your ticket stamped, the better precedence you receive when boarding. That would make sense, right? Turns out that's not the case. It is so much *not* the case that I'm willing to admit that I have never been more wrong about anything in my entire adult life.

    We huffed our cumbersome and over-packed luggage from our Upper West Side apartment down through the treacherous reaches of the B-D-F-M to the Grand Street stop and made our way west to the corner of Canal and Allen around 7:45 p.m. Still under the blissful illusion of arriving early, we heaved our luggage across crowded and compact sidewalks, talking with joyful enthusiasm of the Thanksgiving family traditions we would soon be immersed in. We were mid-laugh when we made the final turn onto Canal Street, and the joy dropped quickly out of voices. Before us lay a horrifying and grizzly scene as a clogged, congested mass of people surrounded the office entrance of the Jaguar bus line. A mass growing larger by the minute.

"Fuck," Erin sighed.

And fuck was right. How we didn't anticipate that a whole slew of equally poor and underprepared travelers would also be braving the harsh, late-November weather to try and get home is beyond me. Thanksgiving is the busiest travel time of the year; of course, there'd be others doing whatever is necessary to get from New York City into the heartlands of America to see their families. Even using the assumption that some of these travelers would be taking different buses at different times, the numbers of the horde were staggering. We immediately felt in over our heads.

Despite the growing sense of unease and against our better judgment we braved our way into the office/makeshift refugee camp. Crossing the threshold, the lobby was littered with bodies sleeping on and in any spare luggage that would accommodate them. More were splayed corpse-like and distressed across any flat surface they could occupy. The lucky ones—if they can be called that—commandeered the folding chairs that lined the vestibule; at least they had some cushioning to support them. All appeared as though they had been living out of this lobby for weeks. From somewhere in the deep, a sustained scream from a panicked baby reverberated off the walls and refused to be ignored. Travelers, desperate for warmth, were smothered with spare garments from torn open suitcases. Children, seemingly bred into this captivity, ran around aimlessly and unsupervised, kicking, screaming, and punching with wild abandon. The sick and the elderly were mostly relegated to the backmost corner, away from the general population. They huddled mournfully next to a trophy case—a cruel irony if ever there was one. Anxiety and fear rendered me incapable of investigating why a trophy case was even there in the first place; it certainly wasn't to showcase their safety awards.

As Erin and I made our way through the human detritus to the ticketing counter in the back, we were careful to avoid any outstretched hands or pleading eyes, knowing no one could help anyone in this situation. Behind the ticketing counter, a young Chinese girl, no more than about sixteen, sat glued to her phone with a calm, slightly bemused expression. That she could remain in such repose while surrounded by unparalleled bedlam was, quite frankly, unnerving. She didn't look up as we approached. Erin and I waited patiently for her to finish texting or playing a game on her phone. It felt like interrupting her would be a dangerous thing to do. During a brief moment, when she looked away from her phone, Erin and I presented our pre-printed bus tickets to her. With our dreams of early boarding obliterated, our faint hope was that these printed letters of transit would secure safe travel and perhaps a few meager rations. That was mistaken assumption number two.

We learned quickly that validation and documentation are frowned upon in the world of Chinatown buses. Presumably, this has to do with the nature of the endeavor: random strangers, crossing state lines, luggage that is neither checked nor screened for illicit substances or illegal contraband, etc. But we innocents did not know this, and the disdain we received from that young girl for presenting these tickets filled me with such humiliation that I all but buried my head in shame. She scanned over the crumpled, loose-leaf sheet of paper on her desk that contained a handwritten list of names. Using an enormous permanent marker, the girl crossed two thick red lines through our names with what I would call an unsettling amount of enthusiasm. She then extracted two small square sheets of paper from a shoe box on the counter with the words Louisville and the number 4 scrawled angrily across them and then went back to her phone. My memory is not perfect, but I am confident we exchanged *zero* words during the entire encounter. No greetings, no clarifications. Nothing. I would be surprised if I was told we even made eye contact at any point during the ticketing process. It was strictly transactional. And we were thankful.

In the moments after, the glaring differences between this mode of transportation and, say, air travel, began to crystalize. With air travel, the goal, in theory, is to try to make your trip and your experience with the company providing the trip pleasant. However, these companies understand the interplay between customer experience and profit. They have whole departments dedicated to discovering the maximum amount of money they can extract from a customer while providing the bare minimum satisfaction to said customer while telling you that your safety and comfort are…yada, yada, yada. It's a genius play, really. All the gripes, complaints, and dissatisfaction that inevitably follow a policy change or a price hike are dealt with on an individual level by the company's customer-facing employees, or they're offloaded to some customer service department that never has to interact with customers face-to-face. We have all gazed passively as countless stewardesses and ticket takers were berated. We've secretly listened to strangers hurling obscenities over the phone to distant customer service representatives. In a really sick way, the fact that we have the opportunity to act this way—to scream, yell, and curse at whoever we want because we're paying for a service—is positioned as a perk that these companies are offering. They push and prod and pressure you until you're about to pop and then pay someone to deal with your bullshit, all while they charge you *more* for that seat they just altered to have *less* legroom.

    Chinatown buses, on the other hand, don't give a fuck about your customer experience. They don't even pretend to. They don't have to. What are you going to do about it? They know the only reason you're there is because you aren't willing or aren't able to pony up the extra money it takes to travel a different way. They aren't going to spend their money on some frivolous customer service department or invest money in increasing customer satisfaction. They are going to let you suffer because they can. You'll keep coming back, time and time again. That's sort of the brilliance of the whole operation. Even if Erin and I were to raise an objection about something, anything, where would we go? The only person with any appearance of authority was the girl behind the counter, and I wasn't about to tempt my life with another interaction with her. If there were any other employees of the Jaguar Bus present, they had been drowned long ago in the vast sea of polluted humanity, quickly overtaking the lobby and spilling out onto the sidewalk outside. Our current situation was so depraved that questions like, "How will we know which bus to get on?" or "Will there be overhead storage?" seemed elitist to the point of insanity—there was a woman propped against the window sleeping with her arms stuffed into the legs of sweatpants; I'm not going to be the guy asking about leg room.

Erin and I jointly decided that the three hours it would take for the bus to arrive would surely kill us if we remained in the vicinity of such carnage, so we took off down the street in search of sustenance and strong drink. I have been told by people in the know that Chinatown has some of the best food in the city. Perhaps, if I were taken there by a local or someone who knows where those places are, I might be inclined to believe them. As it stood, Erin and I were stranded and alone. Each place looked as equally grim and unwelcoming as the last. After a fraught 20 minutes of indecision, we were mercifully delivered to the hilariously titled Pies' N Thighs, a southern comfort food restaurant specializing in handmade pies and hand-dipped thighs. It was there that Erin and I ate as if it were to be our last meal on earth. We consumed chicken biscuits slathered in honey and hot sauce, devoured crisp and crunchy fried chicken that oozed with juicy flavor, gobbled mac'n cheese as thick and creamy as a good lover, and dined on coleslaw more flavorful than any I have ever had. We shoveled all of it and more into our desperate gullets. We ordered round after round of drinks as we tried to supplant the horrors we had subjected ourselves to. We decided that if we were forced to endure this overnight baptism, it was best to do so while interred in a food coma or by being blackout drunk.

    Around 11 o'clock, we slinked our way back to the cattle pen, well-fed and liquored up. We had only been clinging to the side of a wall for a few minutes when a bus pulled up to the curb and opened its doors. The horde descended. The instant the luggage bay doors underneath the bus were opened, people from all distances began tossing and throwing their bags into the depths of that steel beast. It was akin to a Black Friday stampede, the way people trampled over one another to throw their luggage recklessly underneath and then scramble aboard the bus. The display was a horrific disregard for humanity and social norms, and it was absolutely astonishing. The only thing that could have made the scene of savagery worse was if an identical-looking bus were to have pulled up directly behind the first less than a minute later, which it did.

"Aww, fuck! What is *this* fucking bus?" Demanded a woman holding two children at the waist and attempting to sling another bag of luggage under the first bus with her foot. She was not alone in her concerns. The confusion spread like a shockwave through the crowd as people began shouting and cursing and searching for anyone who could provide answers.

"No! No! No! No! No! No! No! No! No!"

Through a thick cloud of cigarette smoke, an elderly Chinese man with thin glasses and a fading hairline emerged to command the mass of humanity, still throwing their luggage beneath the first bus.

"This bus four!" He shouted to a growing number of stunned onlookers. "You no go bus four!"

The mass halted at his words as about half the swarm now realized they had been throwing their luggage beneath the wrong vessel. Then came the frantic and collective shouts as they began rummaging through the bowels of the bus, looking for recently discarded cases and bags.

"You no go Furjinya! This bus four!"

"Lueyfull! Bus Four! You no go, bus Fhive!"

The elderly man commanded everything as he marched amongst the chaotic legion, smoking and screaming. There was a stoicism about him that radiated through the crowd. His gait and demeanor depicted a man who had seen great tragedy in his life. Tragedy he had overcome. And he wasn't about to lose control of a situation like this.

"No! No! No! No! No!" The man would scream in face after face as people attempted to decipher which of the equally unmarked buses went to Virginia and which one went to Louisville. On a blind faith tip from a merciful stranger, Erin and I barreled for the first bus, threw our bags underneath like seasoned veterans, and scampered up the steps of the bus as the chaos on the sidewalk continued.

The interior of our Van Hool c2045 bus was quintessentially utilitarian. The blue, two-by-two seat pairs with gaudy Vegas-themed upholstery showcased neon-tinted roulette wheels and Aces of Spades that reflected awkwardly in the dim light. The seats themselves are angled at an inhospitable 120 degrees, which is reclined far enough to feel that you aren't sitting straight up but not enough to be enjoyable. You are essentially locked into a stress position that requires a near-constant flexing of one's abdomen in order to keep the head and neck in any sort of usable position. There was a noticeable stench attached to each headrest that, despite my best efforts, was impossible to place. With a seating capacity of around 50 and a group outside the bus that numbered at least twice that much, this trip seemed like it was going to be a crowded affair.

On the way down the aisle, we passed a thin, fidgety,

middle-aged Asian man with a wispy goatee sitting alone in the first pair of seats. There was already a line for the bathroom by the time we boarded, which confirmed that its use was absolutely out of the question for the entirety of the trip—any restroom-related problems during traveling would have to be our cross to bear. We found two seats next to each other about halfway down on the right-hand side and staked our claim next to an elderly couple who gave us weak, accommodating smiles as we sat down. They were dressed as if they had either just finished Salsa dancing or intended to do so immediately after they arrived at their destination. Knowing the first stop on the bus trip was at least ten hours away, their outfits and possible holiday plans made them an incredibly endearing and interesting pair.

It was roughly 45 seconds after Erin and I sat down and failed to make ourselves comfortable that we heard the first inklings of dissent brewing. We tried to convince ourselves this was just the perfunctory grumblings of an angry passenger before traveling—here's always one. But the noise from the front of the bus persisted. We tried to ignore it. Everyone did. But there was no way. It kept growing louder. Soon, it appeared that everyone on the bus sensed the same level of discomfort Erin and I did. There was a concerted effort of clutching purses and backpacks close to our person; mothers tried quieting children, some just brightened the screens of their phones in an attempt to capture the child's attention.

Our friends across the aisle looked as disturbed as we did. The woman had closed her eyes and was now holding tightly to her rosary as the decibel levels jumped from disturbance to dangerous.

At the front of the bus, an argument had ensued. Like the rest of the creatures on the bus, Erin and I were forced to witness the impossibly frantic screaming match between the older, cigarette-smoking man from earlier and the wispy-bearded, middle-aged man from the front of the bus. *What* the altercation was about is of the least concern. The amount of unrestricted vitriol these two men hurled at one another was astonishing. My mind cannot comprehend what these two people could have been disagreeing about that requires as much intensity and energy as these two men put into yelling at one another, but snippets of the incidents from Wikipedia flooded my panicked mind. The assumption is that the conflict revolved around a misplaced ticket or a fraudulent claim by the wispy-bearded one. Whatever it was, it was enough to start a verbal onslaught that pinned me, Erin, and the rest of the onboard lemmings to the back of our seats, grim with anticipation of unexpected horror.

Their war was one that started with quick-fire shots, a loud scream that would cut the other one off mid-sentence, and then the opponent would return the volley with a mid-sentence scream of their own. Then the other. And then the other. Back and forth. As the hostility of the argument increased, the distance between the two combatants decreased until the two men were mere inches apart, rage-spewing hatred into each other's faces. The woman who may or may not be prepared for salsa dancing was absolutely beside herself, and she kept whispering what I believed to be prayers into the cross around her neck. I'm not a religious man, but I'd be lying if I didn't say I considered converting while aboard that bus.

Lesser men, surely, would have surrendered to the thousands of insults, taunts, and humiliations these two men must have been hurling back and forth at each other, and physically attacked their opponent. But these were not lesser men. These were titans on the brink. And they were at war. A war in which weapons were sharp-edged words and striking hand gestures, shields were upturned chins and resolute shoulders. Their armies were measured against how many breaths they *didn't* take while launching wave after wave of onslaught onto their adversary. Weaker generals and lieutenants tried to come to the old man's aid, but they were brushed aside. This was the old man's war, and he didn't need their help. He wasn't going to yield to some wispy-bearded filtered cigarette smoker, who may or may not have a ticket. The old man wanted complete and total victory. So staunch was his desire for victory that the elderly man, in a particularly heinous display of hostility, was witnessed, on at least one occasion, using chemical weapons. Out on the sidewalk in front of the bus, after what appeared to be a progress-making détente, the elderly man drew down a deep drag of the lit cigarette in his hand and then, spotlighted by the harsh incandescence of the neon above, exhaled the noxious odor directly into the face of his wispy-bearded opponent. Whatever peace we innocents had hoped for dissipated into the cold November night like the cigarette smoke billowing off the young man's face.

Have I mentioned this entire fight was in Mandarin? I don't think that I have.

Finally, after pushing his way through an aisle filled with babies and bags and purses and pillows, the old man, tailed angrily by the wispy-bearded man, pointed at an unoccupied seat, screamed one last syllable, and then turned to walk off the bus. It ended the war with what many passengers, myself included, thought was an acceptable cease-fire. The young woman from earlier, still glued to her cell phone, then came on board and began counting heads. However, the middle-aged opponent, apparently unsatisfied with his accommodations, attempted to take up the war again and began screaming and chasing after the old man up the aisle. It was an action that resulted in a unified release of disgust from the entire congregation of onlookers. Just as the middle-aged man reached his nemesis, the older one turned around and ended the last-stand effort by thrusting his index finger vertically in the air, then pointing to the man, and finally pointing back to the seat. In the silence that followed, the elderly man exhaled deeply and then walked off the bus.

Like almost every other question about this situation, why this particular gesture was enough to pacify the man will, unfortunately, go unanswered. But it worked. The middle-aged man settled into his seat, and at 11:23 p.m. Eastern Standard Time, the Jaguar bus pulled away from the curb and headed off to Louisville, Kentucky.

As we rumbled from state to state over a never-ending tarmac, I tried desperately to ease myself to sleep, but my thoughts were continuously apprehended by one nagging question: who is driving this bus? Again and again, my mind moved toward the safety and aptitude of the person tasked with captaining this bus to its destinations. How can a person ever become qualified to handle this type of torture? Right around the seven-hour mark of our journey, I started to get concerned for the driver's health and our safety. He appeared to be the same driver that was present with the bus when it pulled up, but the fact that someone could be subjected to making a trip like this more than once a day has to be illegal, right? I've had flights canceled because a pilot didn't get his recommended eight hours of shut-eye; this guy's running back-to-back on a baker's dozen worth of hours per trip? I couldn't see well from my vantage point, but it looked like the driver's head was nodding a little more than the road bumps should elicit. After three or four excursions onto those annoying rumble strips on the sides of highways, I found myself extremely grateful they were there to wake the driver up from his little catnaps behind the wheel.

Even with the driver's intermittent narcolepsy, I didn't know real fear on this trip until we pulled off the highway and into a crumbling parking lot behind an Elks Lodge on the outskirts of who-the-hell-knows. After wheeling the bus up across a few of the empty faded parking spots and shifting the metal beast into park with a forceful wrenching of his arm, our driver stood up out of his seat, jacked open the doors, and walked off the bus.

No warning, no notice. Not even a quick check on the passengers or a note for whoever was going to find us in this random Elks Lodge parking lot. He didn't even look at us. He just walked off. Not to an awaiting car in the parking lot, not into the Elks lodge, he had no discernible destination. He walked across the parking lot, out onto the sidewalk along the road, and then just kept walking on into the distance until he finally disappeared from our lives as mysteriously as he had entered. If the small number of riders that were still awake at that hour were as terrified as I was by the whole event, they showed no signs of it. I was sweating and alone.

I sat there, consumed by my anxiety in that abandoned parking lot, until the screeching of hot tires on asphalt brought me back to reality. Out of the front window of the bus I saw a small green Miata tear around the corner of the Elks Lodge and skid into an imaginary parking space about ten feet away from the bus. A taught Asian man dressed in a denim jacket and khaki slacks exited the convertible, snubbed out a cigarette with the heel of his boot, and boarded the bus. He gave a weak, disconcerting look at the new crew he would be captaining. From atop the dashboard, he picked up a clipboard and scanned over it. Apparently finding no use for it, he tossed the clipboard to the side and began marching down the aisle of the bus, counting heads (it's important to point out that he was not checking tickets or names; he was simply making sure the body count was correct). Our new captain counted until he reached the end of the bus, then turned and sprinted back to the front at full speed. Back at the front of the bus, the man turned around to face his prisoners. After an interminable ten seconds, he bent down a little, extended a thumbs up, and shouted, "Yeah!" He ratcheted the bus into gear, navigated us out of the parking lot, and pulled us back onto the highway. His exaltation and the swishing his khaki pants made as he sprinted up the aisle of the bus were the only noises I heard him make the entire trip.

    I don't remember much after that. I slept through the majority of the rest of the trip, waking sporadically as we pulled into each stop on the route. I do remember *feeling* the rest of the trip, though, every bump in the road, every jerk of the wheel, every smell wafting from beneath the bathroom door or out of a sweaty armpit. Everything about this journey tore further and further into the fibers of my humanity until the bus finally pulled into a strip mall on the outskirts of Louisville. It was hard. I had been hurt and abused. I felt powerless in my efforts to protect myself and my girlfriend from the nightmare we found ourselves in. Erin didn't say anything, but I knew she could feel it—something had changed within me. We had endeavored upon this trip and had seen and done things that could not be undone or unseen. We were a part of it now. We were accomplices. Exiting the bus into the harsh reality of morning held no pleasure of escape, for we knew after our short 72 hours in Louisville, we would once again have to face our abuser for the 13-hour bus ride back to New York City. At that moment, I can honestly say there were serious doubts about my ability to endure the return journey. Standing on that sun-blistered asphalt, my resolve at an all-time low, I answered for the first time the question I would be asked countless times in the future. Will this kind of torture and humiliation be enough for me to change my ways and finally live a better life? I don't know.

    Probably not.

TUESDAYS IN LEXINGTON

It's strange the way things turn in a restaurant. The tables, both literally and metaphorically, are turning all the time. This week's special turns into next week's push. Strangers turn into customers, who turn into regulars, who turn into nuisances. And out the window, summer turns to spring, spring turns to fall, and so on. All of the turns in the life of a restaurant create a cyclical feeling, an expectation you can depend on—for better or worse—to get you through the otherwise grueling life in the service industry. With that expectation, you know that Thursdays are going to be busy because it's two-for-one drinks; you know that the food is going to get backed up on Tuesday nights because the B-team cooks are working in the kitchen, and you know that the new girl with no experience is going to cry at least twice in her first week and you're *not* going to feel sorry for her because nobody felt sorry for you on yours.

These consistencies give you protection, and when something impacts that protection or breaks it completely, you inevitably feel a piece of yourself break with it.

Tuesday day shifts as a bartender are not overly complicated. You open the bar and 'set up,' which basically just means cleaning. You get ice for the coolers, cut some fruit, and restock from the night before, and since the night before was a Monday, it's not too much heavy lifting. You handle the few daytime lunch customers that choose to sit at the bar, and you wait till the regulars show up around 4:30 for happy hour, serving them their usual Buds and Bud Lights, and you ride out the rest of your shift till you can punch out and get your post-shift cocktail. And that's how it goes. Day in and day out. Month after month. Season after season. But there was one particular Tuesday that was different.

Part of me knew it was going to be different when I woke up. Nothing strange or out of the ordinary, but there was a feeling that something was off. I chalked it up to the fact that I was covering for a girl who had just recently been fired, bad juju and all that, but also, I had just got back from an incredible weekend in New York, so the last thing I wanted to do was bartend on a Tuesday. But I pushed through because that's what you do in the service industry. I went about the usual routine, cleaning and restocking, making small talk with the assorted vendors that dropped by. Everything felt normal. Then, right around noon, I heard a cavernous, rust-tinged drawl call out my name.

"Whadya say, Adam?"

The greeting called me away from the twosome I was serving at the far end of the bar. Not recognizing the voice or the person it was coming from, I went over for a handshake and a closer inspection. Before me was an unmistakably Southern man dressed in a weathered pair of blue jeans and a well-worn black T-shirt. His goatee was a stretched-out bundle of steel wool, a hood ornament on a face that was sun-beaten to the color of a dirty penny. He looked like he fully lived every second of his nearly 50 years.

Sensing my hesitation, the man asked if I recognized him. I didn't. But that's customary for a bartender. By nature of the work, most of the people we meet are drinking. Sometimes a lot, sometimes a little. But because they're drinking and we're not (usually), they tend to recall things differently than what the truth is. We got to talking about who he was, and I slowly began to recall the man standing before me.

His name was Doc.

Doc had been in the bar some months before when his wife was at Good Samaritan, the hospital across the street from the bar. He came into our restaurant for lunch one day and, for some reason, had fallen in love with the place. It was slow the day he came in. The waiter and I needed a healthy distraction to keep the boredom at bay, so I guess we talked to him more than he probably was expecting. I don't know, but we ended up talking with this guy while he slugged down about a baker's dozen of Miller High Lifes and told us stories about his biker bar back home with penny pitchers, random bar games, and a stage that he could play his music on. He told us about his musical tastes. His favorites, as you might have guessed, were Waylon Jennings, Johnny Cash, and Johnny Crocker, but he also had the surprising addition of Louis Armstrong. He told us all about his wife and why she was at Good Sam, and how, back home, people either call him Doc or Two Feathers (apparently a Native American name he received down in Frankfort). He told us a lot, but that's not an uncommon occurrence at the bar top.

Before he left that day, we gave him a shirt from the restaurant for no reason other than we had one. But it seemed to mean a lot to him. Doc clutched that shirt with a look of pride that, to us, seemed entirely inappropriate for the circumstance, but it was nonetheless endearing. He polished off the last of his High Life, bade us goodbye, and took off back to the hospital.

I didn't see him after that, but his name lingered around the bar on the tips of peoples' tongues the way that only really peculiar customer names can. People in the restaurant business love to gossip; rarely does a person like Doc escape unscathed. But we're also easily bored. After a few days, another customer of equal or lesser story-telling worthiness replaced him.

When he showed back up at the bar the second time, I

didn't think much of it. I, especially, didn't think much of why he was here the first time. If I had, I would have been able to avoid an incredibly awkward exchange.

"It's me, Doc. Remember? I was up here a couple months ago because my wife was in the hospital?"

"Oh yeah, how's she doing?" I asked.

"Well, she passed away a while back, man. Now they got me up here at Good Sam. They just diagnosed me with cancer, man. Say I got four months. You got a light?"

The transition was abrupt and startling. He pulled out an abandoned cigarette butt and held it between his fingers. Feeling a little disgusted with myself, given the circumstances, I handed him a lighter and a cigarette, which he immediately lit.

"Can't smoke in here, Doc." I called out to him from across the bar.

The irony of telling a man named Doc, who had just been diagnosed with cancer, that he couldn't smoke inside a bar, was not lost on me.

"Well, here, man. Step outside with me so I don't have to throw it back to ya."

There's a general rule in the industry that speaks to not crossing the bar for strangers. It usually doesn't end well. But it felt different this time. Also, he wasn't quite a stranger. Against a conflicted conscience and under the judgemental gaze of my co-workers, I followed him. We stepped outside, and he surrendered himself onto one of the patio tables and started in on his diagnosis, unprompted.

"I just don't even know, man. I'm not even 50, man. They said I got four months. Four months!" He unleashed a deep cloud of Marlboro Light.

"I just put my wife down a couple months back, man. Say it's all over my body. It's in my fuckin' liver, my fuckin' pancreas, my stomach. Everywhere, man."

He took a long, purposeful drag off the cigarette he was holding in his trembling hands.

"Ain't nobody been up to see me yet. My kids ain't come, my family ain't come. Nobody, man. I love this place, man. I had a blast last time I was up here. I still got that shirt hanging up on my wall. I do!" He said, speaking through a half-smile.

He continued on, and I listened as best as I could, but mostly, I remember thinking about how unprepared I was to talk to a man who was dying. I guess I assumed in that situation questions would come to me, talking points would emerge, jokes to tell, stories to recall, *something*. But when the expectancy is four months, you can't really talk farther than the moment you are in, and this moment was hard to talk about.

"So what's the plan?" I asked after a momentary lull.

"I ain't got no plan, man. Ain't got no time. Them doctors say I got four months to live."

We sat in silence again, and he asked for another cigarette.

"Man, I would kill for an ice cold beer right now, but I ain't got nothing on me but this damn insurance card. They got everything over there at the hospital. They still got this IV in my arm, man."

A bandage was wrapped tightly around his upper forearm, and he kept tapping at it while he was talking.

"They told me, and I said, 'man, if you don't let me out of here and go smoke a cigarette and see my buddies over there at the Tin Roof, I'm outta here. You better let me.' I had to beg three or four of them doctors to let me out, man." He was feigning courage he didn't have—not so much telling a lie, but telling a story in which he has courage and control to subvert a reality in which might not feel like he had neither. I went inside and got him an ice-cold Miller High Life, feeling it was the right thing to do at the moment. I remembered what he drank from the last time he was here, and that turned his thoughts for a second.

"You know it, man. You know me." He grabbed the beer with a smile.

In the absence of anything meaningful to say about the situation, I was desperately trying to remember any facts about his life that I could bring up to talk about instead. I asked him if he was still playing music.

"Yeah, man, that's how I got here. I was up on stage and I collapsed and they brought me down here, man." He took another deep drag of his fourth cigarette since we'd been outside. "Man, I would do anything to sing some karaoke right now, man. You put on some Waylon or Johnny Cash or Louis Armstrong…"

"…Louis Armstrong? Really? Those names don't usually come up together," I said with a laugh.

"You better believe it, man. You put on 'It's a Beautiful World' and I will liven this place up quick…"

A part of me wanted to play the song for him. A worse part of me wanted to correct a dying man about saying the wrong song title. But I did neither. I changed the subject by telling him about a record I had just bought with Louis Armstrong and Ella Fitzgerald, *Ella & Louis*, and he gave a weak smile.

"I just don't know, man. Don't forget about me, Adam, man. I love you, man. Ain't nobody been up to see me. I got 15 children, 11 grandchildren. Just put my second wife in the ground, man. Ain't nobody been up here yet."

He was looking through the bottle in his hands when the tears began to appear. They swelled but never crested the eyelid. They just stayed there pooling and dispersing and re-pooling, over and over. Too proud to break, too scared to subside.

"Do they know? Your children, I mean." I asked him.

"They know, man. They just ain't come down."

"Just ask them."

"I ain't asking them. If they ain't come down, I ain't gon'

do it to make 'em feel sorry for me."

"Well, what's worse, you making them come down because you made them feel sorry? Or you being sad because they never came?"

"I am sad, man."

"I know you are. I think you should call them up."

"You're right, Adam."

He gazed off and took another deep drag. It doesn't matter how tough you think you are; nobody wants to end their life alone. Everyone wants to reach the end and have something to look back on. Something to see and prove they mattered to someone, somehow. Something to provide the reassurance they were alive and they mattered. He re-lit my final cigarette off the dying embers of the previous one and drank the last gulp of his beer.

"I don't know, man. I love this place. I love you, Adam. Don't you forget about me, man. Don't do it. Don't you do it. When I die they are going to take me home to Frankfort. Harrod's Brothers Funeral Home, out there in Frankfort, man. When you hear about it you come up there, man. You pack up a bus load of you guys and you come drink some beers out there with me, man. Don't forget about me, man. I love this place."

He pulled out two of his business cards and handed them to me.

"You keep these man. I still got a penny that I found

when I was up here the last time, man. You take it, man, and you hold on to that. I would kill for another beer and some of those hot wings man. You guys got the best I'd ever had."

He shook the empty bottle. He reached out a hand and took mine firmly when I extended it.

"Don't forget me, man. You're a good dude, man. I love ya, brother."

Then he got up and walked to the swinging exit doors of the patio.

"Don't forget me, man. I'm in Room 438. Don't forget me, man. I love ya, dude." He called out as he crossed the street. And then he was gone.

I sat there for a minute after he had left. Not really thinking, not really doing anything. I'd like to say that I was processing what had just happened, but I wasn't really doing that either. I was just sitting there. After a while, I got up. I went behind the bar, pulled out our staple gun, climbed on top of a barstool, and above the seat he was sitting the last time he was there, I stapled his business card above the bar and wrote, 'Doc's Spot' across the top and shoved that penny underneath the bottom corner of a license plate hanging on the wall. It seemed that it was the only respectable memorial I was able to give to him.

How does one return to a bar shift, let alone a Tuesday bar shift, after something like that happens? I don't know. But I did. Other things happened: the customers came and went, the regulars shuffled in for their cheap happy-hour beers, and all the while, I kept turning over in my head, *"Don't forget about me, man."* Over and over, that southern drawl kept up like a skipping record in my head.

About fifteen minutes before my shift ended, I put in an order of hot wings and ranch to-go. Once I was off, I poured myself a stiff bourbon-ginger ale. I called my girlfriend and retold the story of what had just happened, not fully believing it myself. I told her I was going to take these wings over to him at the hospital. I played out all the scenarios for her. "Either he's lying and he's not there and I get free wings. Or he's lying and he's there and he gets free wings. Or he's telling the truth, he's actually dying and he's not there, in which case, I get free wings again. Or he's telling the truth and he's there, he gets the wings, and gets to see someone he knows brought him something." She agreed.

I walked over to the hospital and told the lady at the counter that I was there to see someone. She just gave me a small nod, never looking away from her computer. I found the elevators and pressed up to the fourth floor. I made my way to the information desk and told them I was there to see a patient. She asked for the room number, and I told her it was 438.

"Gone."

Off to my left, a squat male nurse with his hands in his pockets and his head tilted back, was staring directly at me.

"I'm sorry?" I asked.

"He's gone. Discharged him earlier. He went on home."

"Oh."

The nurse gave a few slow nods of his head and then turned off down the hall.

Looking back now, I wish I had asked more questions about what happened or what was going on, but I don't know if it would have done anything anyway. Waiting for the elevator down, I remember looking out the window as a nurse was crossing through the backlot of the hospital and wondering what I would say if I ever saw Doc again. Would I tell him that I came to see him with wings when my shift was over? Would I tell him that I was thinking about bringing my guitar over so he could play for a little bit if he were going to be stuck in the hospital? Would I confront him about it? Was I lied to?

I don't know, and in the end, it doesn't matter. I walked home, feeling confused and lost and hurt and uncomfortably relieved. I could sense the circle of familiarity being repaired, the shield of predictability and comfort being re-forged around me, and it felt like everything was melting back to normality. And when everything's said and done, Doc finally did get his wish: I never forgot him.

***

AUTHOR'S NOTE: This piece was originally published in 2017 and written, for the most part, in early 2015. In August of 2021, I searched the internet for any information regarding Doc and his diagnosis. I don't have an answer for why I did that. Maybe I wanted more closure than I had. Maybe I wanted some confirmation about what he was telling me. Whatever the reason, I found what I was looking for. Turns out, Doc outlived his four-month diagnosis in 2015. Sadly, he passed away in October 2020. As a final memorial, I've included the obituary, as I found it, below. Take care, brother.

> Frankfort – Stewart "Doc" Scott Perkins, age 52, passed away on Tuesday, October 13, 2020, at home. Services will be held at Harrod Brothers Funeral Home on Monday, October 19, 2020, at 2:00 p.m. with Rev. Tim Jumpp officiating, assisted by Rev. David Rodgers. Visitation will be held at Harrod Brothers Funeral Home from 12:00 p.m. until 2:00 p.m. time of service.
>
> He was born in Franklin County, Kentucky, on February 16, 1968, to the late Billy Shelton Perkins and Ida Elizabeth Mills Perkins.
>
> He is survived by his fiancé, Jean Harp; children, Joshua Perkins (Victoria Childress), Aarron Augustus Perkins, Summer Perkins, Beth Perkins, Andrea Perkins, Destiny Perkins; brothers, Stephen Sheldon Perkins (Tammy), Ancil Ray Hutchison, Bill Hutchison; sister, Liz Hutchison. He was also blessed with several grandchildren, nieces and nephews.
>
> In addition to his parents, he was preceded in death by his brother, Alvie Collins.
>
> Serving as pallbearers will be family and friends.
>
> In lieu of flowers, expressions of sympathy may be made to the Isaiah House Treatment Center, 2084 Main Street, Willisburg, KY 40078.
>
> Arrangements are under the direction of Harrod Brothers Funeral Home & Crematory.

GOOD WINTER, PART I

My friend Jesse recently asked me to go to a concert with him, and, being myself, my initial reaction was one of absolute jubilation. But then the anxiety-ridden introvert in me kicked in, and my immediate next thought was one of sheer dread. I had already made vague plans with myself to stay in and search for all those cool movies I knew weren't on Netflix; I was going to get some food on the way home from work and have a nice relaxing evening. I have had a somewhat semi-stressful week, kind of. That's enough of an excuse to binge-watch and veg out on the couch. It's lame, but these are the types of situations you find yourself in as you get older. I fought back and forth with myself about how to respond to Jesse's request for a time that was too embarrassing to put down in writing, and, in the end, convinced myself going to the concert was the right thing to do. Besides, earlier in the year, I made a promise to myself to experience new things, and this concert was going to be one of them. I told myself, "Experiences like this one are the reason I live in Manhattan, right?"

Wrong.

Wrong, because the concert was not in Manhattan. I didn't know that when I said yes, and if I had, I probably would have declined the invitation in a really snobby, newly-minted Manhattanite way. So, if the concert wasn't going to be in Manhattan, where is the next logical place that you could hold a concert? Brooklyn, perhaps? Queens? Maybe even New Jersey? These locations are all no-brainers for concerts. Plenty of options for venues, easy enough transportation routes to get to from most parts of New York, and a strong diversity of vibes to match any genre of musician. All I needed to know was which one of those well-suited locales I'd be going to. Turns out, none of them. The concert was being held in the small New York border town of Port Chester. I had never heard of Port Chester, NY, and unless you travel along the New Haven line out of Grand Central Station, I'm guessing you haven't heard of it either.

Quick highlights from the Wikipedia page of Port Chester include it being named "The Restaurant and Entertainment Capital of Westchester County," home of a historic Post Office that was placed on the National Register of Historic Places in 1989, and mention of the deadly Gulliver's Fire in 1974 that killed 24 young men and women at a nightclub. So now we're all on equal footing with respect to Port Chester, NY.

After finding out the concert was going to be in Port Chester, the next logical question is, how does one get there? The answer to that question is layered. The quick answer is that you take the Metro North to get to Port Chester. Easy enough, right? Not if you've never taken the Metro North, and especially not if your only interaction with the Metro North is the random squawking of co-workers saying things like, 'It took me two hours to get from Stamford today! Can you believe that?' or 'Some asshole was on his cellphone in the quiet car. The Quiet Car!' For me, the Metro North is not so much a mode of transportation as it is a statement of choices. Metro-North Riders, or any train dwellers for that matter, are the people who decided at one time in their life that a commute and some living space are better than living within the confines of the city. I vehemently disagree with that position, so whenever possible, I avoid any association with them. Mostly, it just means me being completely ignorant about how around 50% of the people get into the city each day. But today, all of that was going to change.

Jesse and I had resigned ourselves to being train dwellers for an evening, so the first item on the agenda was to find the correct train on the correct track at the correct time in the correct section of Grand Central. We had to go four-for-four on this one. It's a parlay. If you get one of those things wrong, you get it all wrong. To ensure the accuracy of our endeavor, I laid this plan, as I do with almost all of my travel plans, in the capable hands of Erin. She has the uncanny ability not only to locate but to find at least three alternate ways of getting to any place within Manhattan. She instinctively knows every stop on every subway line (I have tested her). She knows the weekend subway schedules as well as the alternate routes to take when traffic is backing up the line you always take. And she is always, *always*, right. Even though this particular location was outside of Manhattan, I knew she could find a way,

I sent her a quick text with the details of the concert. Within minutes of sending that text, she had already sent me back fifteen consecutive text messages indicating the arrival and departure times of all of the trains using the Metro North Line going to or through Port Chester. But as the slurry of text messages berated my phone, I noticed a detail that didn't quite add up. The last train left Port Chester, heading back into Grand Central Station on Friday night at 10:18 p.m. If the show was scheduled to start at 8 p.m. and had a run time of about three hours, there was no way we would be able to make that train home. Thus, we would be stranded in Port like a couple of rogue sailors. The introvert in me was taking over. It had found an opportunity to binge-watch and was desperately clinging to it. The introvert pulled out my phone and sent a quick pre-surrender text to Jesse.

"Hey, man. The last train leaves Port Chester for

Manhattan at 10:18 p.m. There's no way the show is over by then, right?"

The introvert loved that text. Not too excited about not being able to go while still showing enough interest to imply it was a shame that we couldn't go. The introvert assumed this would be the end of the conversation and started thinking about which episode of *30 Rock* he would re-watch that evening, safe and secure on the comfort of the couch. But he was wrong.

"Yeah, some of my buddies went to one of his earlier shows and said that it runs till about 11 p.m.." Jesse responded. "But there's a train that leaves at 12:17 a.m.. You have to look on Saturday morning because it's after midnight." With the introvert wholly defeated and with my fate secured for the night ahead, I began planning on how the hell to make it to Port Chester from my office in the Flatiron building.

Since I had no idea what I was doing, the best plan would be to go straight to Grand Central Station after work and hope for the best. At 5:00 p.m., I left my desk and headed to the lobby to catch the elevator, convinced the night was going to be great. Just before the elevator doors closed, the new intern stepped in behind me.

"Any plans for the weekend?" He asked.

"Yeah, I'm going to see Bon Iver up in Port Chester tonight."

"Aw, that sucks. It's supposed to be like 15 degrees

tonight. Talk about a shit winter, huh?"

Fuck that guy.

Now, if you're a natural introvert like me, there's a long list of things that are scary and intimidating about being in New York City, and being in Grand Central Station during rush hour ranks pretty high on that list. In its cavernous Main Concourse, everything moves at an anxious pace: People coming in, people going out. People sprinting, people crawling, people sleeping. People taking pictures, people talking, people not talking. People stranded, people searching. Flinty-eyed security guards staring menacingly, National Guards staring menacingly at the security guards. Dogs, cats, birds, footsteps, ringing phones, conversations, all bobbing along in the wave of human purpose. I got to Grand Central two-and-a-half hours early, hoping that would be enough time to secure my parlay. After circling the information kiosk in the center of the Main Concourse and deciding that only a moron would think that could be of any use, I stood at the end of a 14-person line at the "self-checkout" ticketing machines. Like most people who don't know what they are doing, I tried to look disinterested and seriously inconvenienced at the same time. This is a great tactic because you can stare at the people at the machines like they are idiots for not knowing how to use them, but really, you are desperately observing their interaction, searching for clues to help you understand what's going on. Fortunately, like most things in New York now, the machines were idiot-proof. I got our tickets quickly and without any error. I made it back to the main hall just in time to have two hours and fifteen minutes to figure out how to get to Port Chester—it was less time than I had hoped for, but it would have to work.

As I learned from my father and every war movie ever made, when you are in unfamiliar territory and under siege from an enemy, head for the high ground. I trekked up the 146-year-old marble staircase, imagining what sort of New York treasures lay at its summit. New York is great like that; it gives you little secrets and surprises in unexpected places, and Grand Central is no different. I reached the top of the beautifully constructed staircase, giddy with excitement over the prospect of a new discovery, and found an Apple Store. That was kind of a bummer, actually, but it is what it is. At least it offers a great view.

The Main Concourse of Grand Central Station is a staggering 275 ft from end to end, stretches out 120 ft wide, and rises 125 ft in the air. All in its 35,000 sq ft of some of the most revered architecture in the city. A departure/arrival marquee flanks it on one side and track entrances on the other. The ceiling has been painted a coy, Robin's Egg blue and depicts the astronomical constellations found in the sky above the plane. Even with its inconsistencies, that ceiling is a magnificent achievement. Imagining how far we've come, not only to recognize those star patterns, but to build up a civilization that is advanced enough to create a structure so that we may reflect those star patterns back to ourselves from an artificial sky as we bounce from train to train, destination to destination, is awe-inspiring. There's a good chance you've seen that black-and-white photograph of the Main Concourse where the sunlight is beaming through the windows, lighting the interior in distinct segmented patterns and turning everyone in the photo into these ghostly apparitions. The photograph is almost 100 years old now, but with the right set of eyes, you can still see the same interior it captured way back in 1930. Regardless of the set of eyes you use to look at it with now, though, one thing remains decidedly unchanged.

It has been said that New Yorkers tend to wear a lot of black, and it's true. And while I understand the practical approaches to the color in a city with eight million people—you'd be a monster to try and wear white around here, especially in the winter months—when viewed from a certain vantage point, it renders us incredibly ant-like in our behaviors. From high up on the balcony, with just a slight un-focusing of the eye, the people traversing back and forth across the concourse floor become a bustling hive of worker ants attentively trying to accomplish their objectives. The woman with the suitcase running to catch her train transforms into a worker ant retrieving food for the colony; the massive circle around the couple taking engagement photos becomes the ants entertaining a domineering Queen; the homeless man, overlooked and abandoned, is treated the same as his ant-self's equivalent. We are in constant motion. We muscle through, brushing shoulders and knocking bags, on our way to do whatever it is that we are doing at any particular moment, most of the time never fully realizing how amazing the city is and how lucky we are to be here in the first place.

Sonder: the realization that each person is living a life as vivid and complex as your own. That's what I was doing up there on that balcony. I found that word on the internet. I have no clue if it's a real word or not, but that's not really the point, either. Sondering—if that's a verb. I watched an Asian woman emerge from beneath an archway on the far west side and followed her, suitcase wheeling all the way across the floor. I watched every interaction, every almost bump in her path, every stutter step. I tried to imagine what she was doing. Late for a meeting? Date? Going to see her kids? Volunteer? Score some drugs? Sell stolen Nazi memorabilia? It sounds crazy, but everything is possible in this city, and all things must be accounted for.

I was deep in my mental machinations when a text from Jesse roused me back to reality. He was asking about our transportation, and I turned my attention to the scrolling departures/arrivals board to my left. Different trains leave from different tracks at different times from different places; that's to be expected. But sometimes trains go to the same place at the same time and then go to different places from that place. Sometimes, different trains go to the same place from different tracks at the same time. Furthermore, sometimes the same train leaves from two different tracks at the same time and ends up at the same location at the same time but from a different direction—at least, that's how it seemed to me. Honestly, it was taking a lot of brainpower to figure out, which is always bad news bears for Adam. Eventually, my brain focused on something that *might* have been right and justified it would have to work, and that's what I settled on. I would love to detail how I came to that conclusion, how I discovered that we would have to take train X to stop Y, transfer to train Z and ride that for 45 minutes to get to Port Chester, but the truth is, I don't remember. I do, however, remember feeling assured in my choice at the time—congratulatory, even—that after so little time (only two and a half hours!), I had *finally* figured out how to navigate Grand Central Station.

    Jesse arrived some minutes later, informed me that I was wrong, and led us in the right direction. It hurt, but I shrugged it off. Once we were securely on the correct train on the correct track at the correct time in the correct section of Grand Central, I pulled out a small bottle of bourbon I had purchased on the way to the train station and passed it to Jesse as the train carried us off to Port Chester, New York.

AN HONORABLE DEATH

My razor just died. In my hand, while I was using it, it died. Its usual soothing purr—that same purr I have heard for most of my adult life—stuttered with a mechanical click and then settled into a slow, dulling whimper. I watched as the life bled out of it. What I initially thought would be cause for frustration over the inconvenience quickly gave way to a demoralizing sense of loss and hopelessness. I knew what was happening, but like most of us, when confronted with the prospect of loss, I refused to accept it. When faced with the inevitability of death, we often choose to ignore the realities and impose our own deluded truths. Frantically, I gave it a few stern shakes, trying to rouse life back into it. *Maybe the cord was tangled, and the electricity wasn't reaching it properly? Maybe the head was clogged?* But I had just cleaned it out recently; *it usually never does this.* Quickly, I turned it off and detached the head, emptying the petty debris that had accumulated in its chambers into the squat, black garbage can next to the sink. It didn't help. Once I turned it back on, the soft whimper returned, a slow, drawling whirr as it attempted to continue to perform its duty. Even in its final moments, this small appliance, with such grandeur and nobility, tried to honor its commitments. We were in the bathroom, and I had the small appliance in my right hand. It emanated its final call and then lay silent upon the hand that held it for so many years.

The razor was a Norelco 6843XL Reflex Plus. It is ergonomically crafted to fit perfectly into the hand of an adolescent, which is exactly what I was when I first received it some ten years ago. Its twin was handed to my brother on the same day. It stood at a magisterial 9.4 inches tall and weighed in at approximately 9 oz. A line from the manufacturer's description: "Norelco's Reflex Plus Shaving System, shaving heads automatically adjust in multiple directions to hug unique facial contours for a closer, more comfortable shave." Unique Features include the patented Reflex Actions® System, Unique Lift and Cut® Technology with Individually Floating Heads and came complete with all of the Norelco Reflex series standard features: LED Charge Indicator Light, Full-Width Pop-Up Trimmer, Automatic Worldwide Voltage, Hair Collection Chamber, Protective Razor Head Cap, Cord & Cleaning Brush, Locking On/Off Switch, and a Storage/Travel Pouch. Its force and clout came from a power cord featuring an 8-hour full charge for shaves in foreign environments—mine had long since lost that ability and must, like a struggling geriatric, be plugged in at all times. The power cord, originally around three feet in length, had stretched to an impressive five and a half feet from years of indiscriminate stretching and torquing. The entry points on the plug, however, were still as vigorous and unyielding as they were the day it was purchased.

My father taught me to shave in the upstairs bathroom of our old house when I was 13 years old. Surrounded by dirty shower towels, half-used toothpaste tubes, and fish-scaled wallpaper, I became a man for the first time in my life. I entered this world of manhood despite my older brother's giddy hazing, spewing the kind of aberrant derision that only an older brother can.

"You're gonna cut yourself and die."

"You're gonna screw it up."

"You're an idiot."

My father watched over me paternally with great patience. He showed me how to quarter-fill the sink bowl with warm water so as to wet the blade before and also to cleanse it after each stroke of the razor. He instructed me on how to apply the shaving cream, alerting me of the fallacy that too much cream will actually hurt you in the end, as the excess cream clogs and dulls the razor's edge. He taught me the subtle art of "up-stroke, down-stroke"—a totally unnecessary technique for a 13-year-old, but was received and studied fully by a grateful son.

After the crash course, my father handed me the razor: a two-blade black and chrome Gillette, which, at that impressionable age, seemed like an Admiral's rapier being passed on from one generation to the next. In my Old Navy tank top and And-1 basketball shorts, I felt humiliatingly underdressed for the occasion. Still, with a calm hand and racing heart, and as the two older Lambert men looked on, I dipped the rapier into the warm bowl and dragged the blades across my *properly* lathered upper lip.

It only took about four or five strokes for me to adequately dispense with the half a dozen or so hairs that had sprouted around the corners of my upper lip. Still, it felt like a great accomplishment, as if I were joining an ancient sect of men. Men who were great, noble, and clean-shaven. And this sect was a fraternity to which I would belong for the remainder of my life, dazzling women and visiting dignitaries with my extraordinary blade skills as the much-deserved spotlight reflected softly off both my medals and slick cheeks and chin.

But I soon discovered that I was not a great prodigy when it came to straight blades. Even though I would parade around the house with bloodied tissue plastered to my face and announce to the family things like, "Don't worry, I'm fine. It's just a little nick from shaving. I'm shaving now. Did you know that?" or "Oh, Brother? Are you shaving yet? *No?* Don't worry. We got our whole lives to deal with this, am I right,

Dad?" My ineptitude at shaving seems to have been something my father noticed as well because it wasn't long after I started he presented me with my first electric razor. Just like that first time, my brother was there, except he too was now a member of the club, having sprouted some small stubbles of his own. By this point, my father had also switched to an electric razor, and if I remember correctly, it also was a Norelco, deep forest green with streaks of crimson and steel, whereas ours was a cold, ocean blue with gray trim. His was a three-top razor, just like mine.

As strange as it is, shaving is truly one of the only things that I can actually remember my father teaching me. I know there were others; there had to be. Any sports-related abilities or techniques I must have learned from him, like catching a baseball or kicking a soccer ball. Throwing a football was an innate ability for the men in our family. This preternatural trait came from my father's lifelong training, so it's okay that I don't remember that—but shaving? I never forgot that. It was the inclusion and togetherness of rituals that bound us together and, ultimately, developed my adoration for the razor. Similar to when you stumble upon the realization you and all the men in your family have the obligation of carrying your family name forward, you are a changed man afterward.

I was a changed man then; we all were. Plus, we were Electric Men now! Harnessing the power of technology in the new age to advance our place in the world with clean, sharp, bump-free faces. True to a proper family hierarchy, my father's razor was the best. Then his two sons, the heir-apparent and the spare, were given identical razors and forced to compete to see who was the most deserving. And while I developed facial hair at an earlier age, and it is much darker and thicker than my brother's, he is still older than me and is thus destined for ascendency, and I am not, even though I am a better shaver. He, on the other hand, has recently taken the title of "most-diabolical beard," in what was an apparent eight-month razor strike.

Shaving also allowed my father the opportunity to further cement his legacy in Markisms. My Father, Mark E. Lambert, aka Hollywood, is an incorrigible and unregenerate insulter. He loves it. It wakes him in the morning and comforts him at night. His affinity for insulting, like most Midwestern dads, comes from a deep respect for a well-timed, well-delivered joke, and the idea of his sons shaving, or more specifically *not* shaving, apparently flooded him with inspiration. His two exalted lines are, "What? Is the razor on strike?" and, "We should put some milk on those whiskers and let the cat lick them off." My father would then produce an abnormally large Cheshire grin and cackle like a lunch table full of popular girls. My father uses those lines often and with great enthusiasm. Neither is particularly insulting, but they are ubiquitous in my father's house, and their expectancy can produce a bit of anxiety unless you're properly prepared. This is usually done by either shaving or—and this was my common rebuttal—responding with, "At least I *can* grow a beard." Juvenile, yet accurate. And yet with each Herculean insult my father would berate us with, I would wonder why I hadn't shaved, and my thoughts would inevitably turn to my razor.

    I had just recently gotten back in touch with my old friend after having been bearded for around five years. I changed the design of my face to a detailed and eloquent Clark Gable mustache because—as I have been told—when you got it, flaunt it. So I did. And my razor helped me immensely. Before that, though, the razor had mainly been used as a beard trimmer, the Full-Width Pop-Up Trimmer bearing the brunt of labor, while the Individually Floating Heads were relegated to clean-up duty on the high cheeks and sporadic unibrow landscaping. But further back, before I was a bearded man, I was in my late adolescence and early twenties, and the razor served me about as faithfully as anyone could rightfully expect. So well, in fact, that this razor, with its Unique Lift and Cut® Technology, actually kept me out of a very prominent conversation in the realm of manhood. Because of the respectful and conscientious duty of this razor, I was never able to participate in the conversation about razor burn. What I had assumed was simply another ostracizing event in my life turned out to be something of a blessing. Rather than converse painfully about the itching and redness associated with that temporary tragedy, I walked, itch-free, with windblown cheeks past all hindrances. For this, I must thank my razor.

This razor has some history behind it. A lot of history, actually, and its passing is not something I take lightly or will soon forget. Its death has produced within me a sense of loss that, inexplicably and rather embarrassingly, I have not felt in some time. Maybe it's because I was there when it happened that this feeling of loss is so crushing. I didn't lose it or misplace it or leave it somewhere. I didn't drop it carelessly on the bathroom floor or slam it against the sink. It died. It ended. I had just finished trimming my hair and was out of the shower when I was shaving with it. I had just recently told my father I still have it and still use it, which shocked him greatly. I explained to him, in a very matter-of-fact tone, that all you have to do is take care of it and clean it and maintain it, and your belongings will last much longer than expected. To be fair, this was also a subtle attempt to show him how mature and responsible I have become. And it was true.

This razor, for better or worse, was one of the things I had taken the best care of most of my life. I cleaned it regularly, always placed it back in a safe spot, and wrapped the cord as sensibly around the body as I could so it would stay in working condition. I was proud of this razor and proud of myself for the way I used and maintained it. We grew up together and developed patterns together. Once I developed a set shaving time in my day, the razor and I developed our own pattern for shaving: starting at the back right cheek, moving upward and across in circles until we got to the chin, then switching and repeating on the opposite cheek. Then, the chin, starting on the right side, working under and over and across to the left, then over and across the front. I would always leave the soul patch and mustache for last because they always provided hilarious formations for facial hair, which I would usually take pictures of and send to my siblings.

I had just finished my right cheek, both up and down, and was halfway through the left when the death rattle screeched out, then slowed to a gentle whirr. I immediately admonished myself for having the earlier thought of switching to a straight razor because I thought it would be a great skill to learn and it would look cool. What was I doing? I didn't appreciate what I had. After the mental flagellation, the next feeling that arrived was disappointment: not in the razor, but in myself. What could I have done differently? What could I have changed to keep this in my life longer? Just a little bit more time, that's all I wanted. I didn't even care about finishing the shave; I didn't need to—who cares about something as irrelevant as aesthetics at a time like this? I just didn't want this to end. I just didn't want this to happen. I just didn't.

But it did. And no matter how much pleading I threw in either direction, nothing stopped the inevitable. After a few ineludible moments, the whispers fell silent. With our pattern incomplete, I tried one last defibrillation to the on-switch. It jumped slightly but then returned to a flat line, and I whispered to myself, "That's enough, now. That's enough."

And it was. And I cried. And I felt sorry, and I felt alone. I felt foolish for saying these things and feeling this way about a razor: an old, courageous, honorable little razor. I took the plug out of the wall, and I wrapped the cord around the body as I had done so many times before and as I will never do again.

Colson Whitehead once wrote, "We can never make proper goodbyes... At some point, you were closer to the last time than you were to the first time, and you didn't even know it. You didn't know that each time you passed the threshold, you were saying goodbye." And although he was talking about apartments, it truly is a universal attribution. Sometime over the last ten years or so, we hit the halfway mark. Maybe it was sometime during high school when the majority of its duty took place when I was using it to shave for prom or clean up before graduation. Maybe it was when I was at college in Lexington or back home at my mom's apartment after I got kicked out of school. Or maybe back in Lexington when I got back in, or down in Dallas when my brother took me in after I got kicked out a second time. Maybe it was when I was scraping around Chicago during the interim or back in Lexington when I finally returned and graduated—I used that razor to trim my beard before graduation. Or could it have been sometime after I moved to New York? Maybe at the sublet on 109th or the place on West End Avenue?

Mathematically, of course, some of those places are ruled

out, but it still doesn't change the fact that this razor has been there with me through some of the most important events in my life. I didn't even recognize that until it was too late.

I haven't told my father yet, and I am unsure whether I will. I don't think it would mean as much to him as I would want it to, and I'd rather not set myself up for that kind of disappointment. But I do want to tell someone. I want to tell everyone. I want to stop strangers on the street. I want to tell the world. I want to tear my vocal cords, screaming, "MY RAZOR JUST DIED! DON'T YOU UNDERSTAND HOW TERRIBLE THIS IS?!" But I know nobody will understand. How could they? My pain, my suffering, and my loss are my own.

I am lucky, though. I did get to say goodbye. We were there together at the end, just like the beginning, and every time in between. I did get to say goodbye. Maybe I didn't say the right thing, and perhaps I didn't say the proper thing, but I did get to say *something*. I got to say thank you.

Some may say it's ridiculous to put this kind of effort into an obituary for an inanimate object. Most, I assume, would think it's irrational to write one at all. But these things, these items that travel through life with us, become much more than what they originally were. Some don't. Some simply remain blow dryers, or chopping blocks, or game consoles. But for the select few that transition from trivial to talisman, it's important to remember them and honor them. It's important to remember who we were when we had them. Because we—like all the great objects that have come and gone in history—will one day cease to be, too, and the best we can hope for is living honorably.

CONVERSATIONS WITH MY BROTHER #2

In the car with my family after Erin and I got picked up from the airport,

Me (to my brother): "Why are you acting so weird?"

My brother: "Well, I ate a bunch of shrimp at Dad's, which I'm allergic to, so I took a Benadryl. Then I had a couple beers, 'cause it's the holidays, but that made me tired so I drank a 5-hour to keep me awake 'cause I wanted to see you. And, now, here we are."

SCENES IN THE STREET

You may not know it, but a lot of the best performances in New York City aren't the ones on Broadway. They're not on Off-Broadway, either. They're not even scripted. The truly great performances are daily tragedies that play out in front of you every day. From a bench in any borough, you can watch—free of charge—as untrained actors in haphazard settings deliver extraordinary performances raw with the existential intensity of daily life.

I was on my lunch break, sitting on a bench around the corner from the bookstore where I work, when I was interrupted by a great commotion. A middle-aged couple stormed past me in apoplectic fury, yanking angrily on lazy luggage and muttering incoherently through gritted teeth. In the heat of the moment, it was unclear if the couple was directing their mutterings toward each other or if some external tormentor was to blame. I watched them as they barreled east toward the crowded intersection at West 82nd Street and Columbus Avenue. It wasn't until the woman's third reprisal of her signature gesture—let's call it a scornful Warrior 1 pose—that the root of the couple's indignation revealed itself in the form of a young girl.

She tore past me, clutching the hem of her black skater dress in her hand, bounding carelessly across the city sidewalk in the direction of the couple. She caught up with them just before they reached the corner of the street and uttered her first objection.

"Why are you leaving?!" Hands now raised in a manner eerily similar to the scornful Warrior 1 from earlier. My immediate thought—*I'm watching the revelation of an affair unfold*—was quickly supplanted. It was clear that this was no lover's quarrel. It was a family drama playing out in real time by real people and it was reaching its penultimate conflict with a frantic pace.

The women exchanged the majority of the dialogue in the scene. Replete with exaggerated gestures and more than a few slapping of luggage handles back into their place. The argument was an endless stream of accusations and explanations from both parties. In only one instance did the man insert his opinion on the matter. After listening to one of the young girl's pleas, the man finally interjected, "I know you had a plan. I know how you wanted it to go, but that isn't what this is. That isn't how it goes. Life *isn't* perfect!"

Unlike professionally produced shows, these scenes in the street are not attended by a quiet, obedient audience. The city and its citizens don't stop for these performances, even when it seems like they should. Even if it seems like this unscripted public performance is the most important experience in these characters' lives, it doesn't stop dogs from needing their walks or prevent people from hustling back to work after lunch. A professional-looking woman in her mid-forties, clad in a slate-colored pantsuit, scampered past the family, grumbling, "These fucking morons are in the middle of sidewalk…" We must all subject ourselves to the rationale that this place is so much bigger than one person or family, even for the ones in a fight.

A toddler pushing her teddy bear in a stroller, its plastic wheels scraping agonizingly against the concrete, obscured the young girl's verbal response to the man's brief but brilliant "Life Isn't Perfect" speech. Physically, though, she responded with that obliterating look of disdain many develop in the early teen years, a weaponized defensive tactic that is the physical representation of "Shut the fuck up. Thanks." Hearing what her body was trying to say, the man rolled his eyes, crossed his arms, and leaned back against the stoop railing behind him in an excruciating exit from the conversation. He remained in the position until finally, with one final disapproving harrumph, he unsheathed the luggage handle he had been so stubbornly smashing throughout the scene and walked off.

With a moment's hesitation, the older woman began to follow his lead. With desperation setting in, the young girl performed her final protestation. Tenderly grasping her mother, hands framing the side of her cheeks, the young girl pleaded, "Stop. You don't have to go."

As tears traced the outline of the daughter's hands, the mother responded, "It doesn't matter. I don't have you anymore."

With this, the child released her hold. She turned away and began back the way she came. The woman stood resolute in the same place for a moment. Then she gathered herself together, clasped the handle of her luggage, strode off east, and rounded the corner.

I don't have you anymore.

God, what a line.

This city shows you stories like this all the time. Anyone who's lived here, and just about everyone who's visited, has a New York City story; they've seen one of these performances. The good ones are when you remain an audience member. The ones where you remain detached and uninvolved in the story, meekly brandishing your "interested observer" status. This is especially true when the stories turn violent, as they can in myriad unexpected ways in the city. Violent or not, though, the performances are prevalent, and you aren't always able to retain your seat in the audience.

On one of my first days in the city, days after Erin and I had moved into our quaint sublet on 109th Street, I took an adventure through the North Woods of Central Park. This section is unlike anything else in the park. It is a place where the picturesque scenes so abundant for romantic comedy backdrops and screen saver selections are replaced with a rugged woodland landscape noted by ardent birdwatchers for its seclusions and solitude. I was walking along one of the tree-covered paths in the North Woods when I came upon a man sitting on the edge of a stone step about halfway up the stairway.

"Hey, man. You got a lighter?" he asked, as I approached.

"Sure," I responded. I pulled a lighter out of my pocket and handed it to him.

"You gotta turn around, though," he said quickly.

"What?"

"You gotta turn around," he repeated.

"Nope."

"Are you a cop?"

"No, I'm not."

"You gotta turn around, man."

"I'm not turning around. Light your fucking cigarette, or give me the lighter back."

"Alright, man. Fuck."

Unfortunately, he didn't light his cigarette. He pulled out

a cylindrical glass tube and burned the far edge and inhaled the crystal amphetamine instead. Then he handed me my lighter back. I stormed off through the path, awestruck and horrified that I just helped a man smoke crack within 48 hours of living in New York City. The trail opened up to a roadway, and across the street, I saw about 200 kindergarteners celebrating a field day on the lawn, waving banners and bouncing balls, laughing and giggling away. It wasn't a part I was expecting to play ever in my life, and certainly not in my first couple of days living in New York City, but you can't always control the role you're cast in.

    Of course, not all the scenes in the streets are tragedies, either. Tiny city miracles happen every day. You play your part as the hapless naivete who gratefully receives your phone from a stranger that's just been left on the cafe table. You play the love-struck fool for things as simple as someone moving slightly out of the way so that you can squeeze in the subway during rush hour. I watched a comedy of errors unfold on the corner of 72nd Street and West End Avenue as a man on a bike was bumped to the ground by a distracted driver. Before the biker could get his bearings, he was surrounded by people helping him up, and a vigilante mob had overtaken the car that hit him, snapping pictures of the license plate and calling the NYPD.

    I once helped a woman pick out a pair of earrings at the bookstore for her co-worker who was leaving. To the chagrin of my managers, we ended up talking for an hour about poetry and the photographer Vivian Maier. Some months later, I saw her on the subway. I had my headphones in, but we made eye contact across the crowded car. She pinched her ear lobe, wiggled it back and forth, and winked at me, then went back to reading her book.

These performances, these moments that make up the stories of your life are—if you'll indulge an English Major his Shakespeare quote—but a walking shadow, a poor player, that struts and frets his hour upon the stage, and then is heard no more. As with our own lives, there is no encore for these scenes in the street. The performances strut and fret their hour upon the stage, and are heard no more. Yet, they stay with us; they reverberate throughout our lives. They influence our thoughts and direct our actions, whether audience or actor.

With my break nearly ending, I left my bench and returned toward work. As I rounded the building on the corner, I looked back just in time to catch the woman hustling back in the direction of their daughter's retreat. Following from the wing and struggling to manage the two large pieces of luggage, the man panted breathlessly behind her, "Honey! Honey…wait up!"

Exeunt.

NOTES ON A CORNER STORE

There is a corner store down the street from my apartment. There isn't much reason to mention this except for 1) I've lately spent a good deal of time thinking about this corner store, and 2) I refer to it as a corner store. Here in New York, the preferred nomenclature is *bodega*.

Bodega is a Spanish word[1] that roughly translates to "warehouse" or "cellar" as far as I can tell, and though they may have had their beginnings in predominantly Spanish-speaking locations, the term has been cast as a catch-all across the city of New York. Historically speaking, bodegas served not only as neighborhood stop-and-shop establishments but also as cultural touchstones for the millions of people, namely immigrants, who call New York City home. More than just

---

[1] If you're interested, you can find a ton of history about the culture of bodegas on the internet. Very much worth a search.

a place to quickly grab a few household essentials, bodegas function as quasi-embassies for the varied ethnicities and backgrounds throughout the city, offering the cuisines, culture, and community to those in need. None of the corner stores I frequent reflect the emotional connection that a bodega provides, so I don't use that term. I say corner store[2]."

With respect to the many other expat Midwesterners (read: white) who have made their home across the city over the past few decades, the word *bodega* resembles a certain line in the sand; once one crosses it, that tends to be the only term that one will use to refer to "the store on the corner" of one's street or that is in close proximity to the place where one works regardless of how stringently it adheres to the bodegas-as-embassy definition. And since it is a colloquialism that is somewhat indicative of New York City, the newcomer[3] who adopts the terms too quickly is, rightly, met with a bit of skepticism[4].

So what are we to make of the recent homesteader who uses the language of the natives recklessly? It depends on a

---

[2] Which I shouldn't feel weird about but I do. As an outsider to the city by birth, using the term corner store when the term bodega could apply feels like it cements my outsider status, only this time it's by choice. Also, there's a lot of gentrification guilt that's tied up into that too which accounts for a good bit of the weirdness.

[3] Especially the younger ones.

[4] And why shouldn't they be? In what context do we view the foreigner who readily acclimatizes themselves to a new environment and adopts the language as a good thing? Hearing the phrase, "I'm running down to the bodega" from the neophyte New Yorker is on par with the lily-white American who says, "Actually, it's pronounces 'qwee-son,' not croissant." It is the epitome of cringe.

few things[5], but generally speaking, it's a vibe thing. Like most things in life, if you're coming at it honestly and not acting like too much of a try-hard, you're probably fine[6].

Well, anyway, back to my corner store. It's located one and a half streets south (or southwest, depending on how accurately you adhere to New York City's 29-degree offset) of my apartment, and it is exactly 178 paces from the entry doorway of my building to the counter at the store, which makes it convenient[7] for quick trips of necessities. It's flanked

---

5 Mainly, though, it's geography. If you live in and/or are in New York, when you use the term bodega, you're not likely to raise any eyebrows. Whether you use the term or not, people are going to know what you're referring to. If someone uses it in a situation that is located outside of the city, there is usually a different result. Likely, the first thing that will happen is that one person will stop the conversation abruptly to ask, *"What the fuck is a bodega?"* The speaker then has two options: they can engage in a way that is constructive to the group, or they can engage in a way that is destructive to the group. The path the person decides to take will say far more about their character than anything else said person has done or said.

Constructive engagement is when the speaker says something to the effect of, "Sorry, corner store." If they are so inclined and the present company is not aware of the speaker's place of residence, the speaker may further their input, for the effect of clarification, "Sorry, that's what they call corner stores in New York." The speaker then shifts the arc of the conversation back to the story that they were attempting to tell.

The destructive engagement is a familiar path to anyone who has been in the presence of a person who loves attention. They will use the *"What the fuck is a bodega?"* prompt to situate the attention squarely on their shoulders for another interminable amount of time and say a lot of really annoying things like, "Well, in New York…" or "According to the Times…" or "I think you should know…" etc.

6 So, a note of warning: if you are around a person who, when asked what a bodega is, uses that time to keep the conversation on them for as long as possible, you are in the presence of a bad person. A quick test for identifying these sorts of people is to focus on the frequency and emphasis of questions responded to that begin with the word *well*. To use the previous footnote example, "*Well*, in New York…", "*Well*, according to the Times…", "*Well*, I think you should know…" One or two *well*'s are permissible, but anything after that and you're going to have a bad time talking to that person.

7 (Note of warning: this footnote is mostly useless and irrelevant to 99.9% of people on the planet. Read at your discretion.) It's actually pretty inconvenient with respect to the traveling terms administered by my first college roommate and me. My roommate and I defined classroom buildings and campus destinations in terms of single-cigarette smokability. We were both heavy smokers at the time, and, like it is with most addicts, cigarettes kind of ran our lives. A close, preferable distance was easily traversed in a

on both sides and above by apartment buildings, which roots the corner store squarely among what could feasibly be 3,000 tenants with grocery and household-essential needs. Luckily enough for the corner store, most, if not all, apartment complexes and housing structures appear to be

cigarette or cigarette-and-a-half's distance from wherever one's starting location may be.

Conversely, a classroom building that was a three-to-four-cigarettes smoked distance away was a nuisance. This distancing was always an approximation—we were not chain-smoking our way to every destination on campus—and it became known as the Melaragni Method. Typical responses using the Melarani Method are, "Umm. It's about a cig or two, depending on traffic," and "How far's the science building? Damn, dude. I don't know—six?"

Because 178 paces fall below the distance of the time it takes to smoke a single cigarette, the proximity of the corner store has become a question of situations more than distance. Since a straight shot—no red crosswalks/no traffic—is 178 paces from door to counter, to smoke an entire cigarette on the way to the corner store, one must decide against a list of variables. The first, if given the free pass across 73rd Street, one may take it and then, after crossing the never-ending Brownstone renovation in front of 270 West End Avenue, may either stand alongside the avenue-facing wall of the corner store, by the free newsletters and brochures and finish their cigarette there. Or, they may continue around the corner, turning east on 72nd Street and finishing their cigarette on the street facing the store entrance on either side of the tree embankment that asks you to politely "curb your dog."

This scenario is the simplest of solutions if no externalities are involved, i.e., people. While I have never had anyone mention, suggest, or gesture any sort of displeasure about the smoke from my cigarette—being that it is New York City, and we live in a fairly residential section of it—I wouldn't put it past someone to chirp at me for smoking too close to them. It's unlikely, but it's an anxiety you develop about smoking and the best way to release that anxiety is by—you guessed it—smoking! (Aren't addictions fascinating!)

The second variable is another path, which is considerably longer yet more preferable when smoking a cigarette. If the crosswalk indicates that it is safe to cross, the smoker may cross and then wait to cross the broader avenue of West End, allowing for extra smoking time. If one has reached the west corner well-timed, one is afforded up to three extra drags while one waits for the crosswalk to administer you across the avenue. From there, one travels south in front of the apartment complex at 263 West End Avenue until you reach the crosswalk at 72nd and West End Avenue, where one has presumably finished more than half of one's cigarette. This path is especially fruitful as 72nd Street is a main thoroughfare in the city. The street lights are not registered to a simple go, slow, stop protocol but operate with a go, slow, stop to all left-turning vehicles, while northbound travelers may continue further for as long as a minute or two, and then stop. After the avenue is cleared of all transportation vessels, one may cross, hopefully with enough time to finish your last drag and throw the cigarette butt into the sewer drain as you step up onto the sidewalk apex of the corner store on 72nd and West End Avenue.

Now, just because one *can* smoke a cigarette every time one wishes to traverse to the corner store, the trip does not require one to do so. But this is the kind of stuff you think about when standing alone at night, ripping a dart outside a corner store in Manhattan.

lived in. My area has graciously been spared from the trend of apartment ownership by the global elite, in which they purchase apartments simply as a safety deposit box—an investment strategy—rather than with any intention to live in them. For every apartment that is purchased but not lived in, that is one less family/customer who will not be around to purchase goods or services from the local restaurant, grocery store, or tailor. As the practice continues, the stores, losing customers, will be forced to shut down. That space is usually then scooped up by chain stores or global corporations who have the money to foot the bill for New York City's egregious rent rates. This process is one of the contributing factors to the "decline in neighborhood sectionalism," where neighborhoods throughout the city are losing their personality in lieu of the homogeneity and ubiquity of the chain store[8].

In that sense, you could say that my specific corner store is a lone reed. A lone reed, standing tall, waving boldly in the corrupt sands of commerce. It is a quintessential small business that may or may not be family-owned—it's hard to tell with the rag-tag group of employees that are running it. It's the topic of a somewhat timid debate between me and Erin about how this ensemble of employees came together[9]. Still, trying to

---

8   Granted, this probably doesn't register as an issue for people outside of NYC. Why would they care if the East Village, or Chelsea, or Dumbo keep the character? But it's important to consider the way that similar processes afflict neighborhoods around the country, not just in the major metropolises.

9   I say timid because the debate is usually just me bringing up the topic again during a late-night beer run or a quick stop to get chips and salsa after the bars, and Erin replying, "haven't we *already* talked about this?"

comprehend that this place on our corner is a "small business" is a difficult concept. It is, of course, small, and, a business, but it is never the picture that is painted by the media when "the struggles of the small business[10]" are espoused. I've never seen a bank commercial for small business loans that matches what I'm looking at when I walk into my corner store. But maybe that's the point.

If I were to look at it objectively, in business terms, this corner store seems like a bad business. And the only real reason I shop there is because it is close to my apartment; it's certainly not because of the prices[11]. It doesn't instill in me a sense of pride that I am supporting a small business—it is just close. Even the deli, usually the saving grace of any sub-par establishment, is bad. The grill is consistently never on, so all hot sandwiches have been abandoned for a regular deli-style sandwich. And to top it all off, the deli is manned by the meanest deli counter dude in all of Manhattan[12].

---

10 Payroll, healthcare, PTO, hiring, business loans, etc.

11 Even in over-priced-everything New York, the prices at most corner stores are absolutely felonious.

12 Seriously, this guy sucks. And the first couple of times I interacted with the guy, I thought it might end up as a kind of Soup-Nazi sort of thing, like Seinfeld, but it didn't. It's just a shitty dude making shitty food, and in order to get that shitty food, you have to wait patiently until he notices your presence and then make serial killer levels of eye contact with him to indicate that, no, I'm not simply waiting in line to pay and am, in fact, requiring of your services. If he chooses to recognize you as a customer, he will begrudgingly put down his cell phone, exchange an exasperated look with the cashier, let out a scoff, and then let his gaze settle upon you while he waits impatiently. If you are ignorant enough to ask if the grill is still on, you will have to wait an additional 30 seconds while he sighs, glances down to the grill, refills his lungs with debased breath, and then responds simply by shaking his head in the negative. You then will look above his head at the hastily scrawled menu and frantically search for a menu item that doesn't necessitate a grill.

After a few interminable seconds pass, you will inevitably decide upon the Italian, the Roast Beef sandwich, or the Turkey Club, as those are the only *true* options left available to you. Given more time,

To be fair, though, the corner store is deceptively well-stocked. The main difference between a corner store and a grocery store, besides the size, is that a corner store appears not to have everything that a grocery store offers; you might think they wouldn't have certain items, but you would be wrong. It's all there. And I'm not just talking about tier-one items like bread, cheese, eggs, butter, and all that; I'm talking third- and fourth-tier items like hoisin sauce, cardamom, cream of tatar, the wild stuff. There are under a handful of items that I have not been able to find at my local corner store that are available at a traditional grocery store, but what they are, I cannot remember. That's sort of the magic about these places. A corner store's greatest strength lies in its ability to store and stash a ton of items that you thought couldn't

---

one may venture into more exciting sandwich territory, but under the pressure constraints of disaffected eyes and frustrated finger taps, those are the only options that will come to mind. The man behind the counter will then ask you, in a voice scarcely above a whisper in an unrecognizable accent, whether you want your sandwich on a roll or a hero roll. The fact that both options contain the word roll is not lost on the man behind the counter, nor do I think he cares which decision you ultimately make, as I have been subjected to both versions despite clearly saying the opposite. He will then grab his bread of choice and coldly turn his back to you while he "prepares" your sandwich behind the counter.

Here, you may find that you have time to peruse the store for a drink and side dish because, inexplicably, those things are not within a ten-foot vicinity of the deli counter. However, you would be wrong. As soon as you muster enough courage and self-purpose to do this, the man will turn his head slightly and seethe something along the lines of, *"cheshhh?"* in your general direction. All plans that had been made to search for chips and a drink will disappear as you frantically attempt to decipher what was just gestured to you. If you take more than a nanosecond to respond, he will turn his head 180 degrees, exorcist-style, and repeat his question louder and more aggressively—*"Cheshhh?!"*

If you are able to keep your bodily fluids and solids intact, you will realize that the question he is attempting to ask you is whether or not you want cheese on your sandwich. I am sure that they offer different kinds of cheese besides American or Swiss, though I have never had the courage to venture a guess (I once saw an old woman have the audacity to ask this deli guy for muenster, and I thought he was going to kill her). You will instruct him which cheeses you prefer, and then the beast will go silent for as much as *seven* minutes while he finishes making your sandwich. Honestly, fuck that guy.

possibly be within a store of its size. The trick is finding them.

For instance, suppose one were to assume that croutons were next to the lettuce or salad dressing or even near other dry goods such as noodles or rice; you would be wrong. If one were to assume that they would be in the aisle with random assorted dry goods like rice cakes or crackers, you would also be wrong. If you were to assume that this store does not have croutons after looking for 15 minutes and not finding any, you would again be wrong. The croutons at my corner store are located at the end of the deli counter facing out, on the third shelf below the seaweed paper and baby food.

This "put-it-where-it-fits" stocking philosophy is not only incredibly cumbersome on the customer, but it also flies in the face of at least 40 years of planographic[13] theory and represents the dividing line between the corner store and the big-box/grocery chain down the street. What those places have that your typical run-of-the-mill corner store doesn't have is money. Money and science, and they use that money and science—plus a good helping of social psychology—to influence your shopping behavior. And they are very good at it. There are entire courses of study about it.

---

13 A planogram, as defined by the English Oxford Dictionary, is "a diagram or model that indicates the placement of retail products on shelves in order to maximize sales." It is the use of a planogram that we have to thank for the odious phrase, "Eye level is Buy Level." It is the type of capitalistic endeavor that seeps into our minds and thoughts without any such awareness of it. Retail science and its practitioners use things like color, floor mapping, and visual product placement to "maximize the retailer's value appropriation across the supply chain." It is the science that revolves around ideals and mission statements that include phrases such as "sensory experience," "distance from unit," and "layout principles to create a 'general flow' that keeps customers efficiently moving through the aisles and spending money."

Notre Dame[14] College Online opens its webpage on *The Psychology Behind a Grocery Store's Layout* under the very phrase, "Welcome to a Sensory Experience." In that section, it details the well-researched and analyzed floor layout of nationwide grocery store chains:

> "The entryway is designed to be inviting so it reinforces a positive customer retail response. Most managers place their sensory departments, including bakery, produce and florist at the front of the store. These departments are known to activate the shopper's salivary glands through sight, smell and taste, which entice them to spend money on things that weren't necessarily on their list. These departments operate on high margins and depend on effectively drawing customers by stimulating their senses."

These three departments are then broken down by their respective duties to the store and the "sensory experience" of the consumer.

> "*Bakery:* The wafting smells of freshly baked breads, cakes, and cookies cause a psychological reaction that makes shoppers hungry, which often

---
14 Go Irish! (*Whaddya say, Vick?*)

causes them to buy more.

Produce: The bright colors of produce excite the eye and tempt the shopper to purchase more produce.

Flowers: The floral department is nearly always located by the entryway as it boosts the store's image in the shopper's mind through the bright colors and fragrant smells."

You're being primed, is the gist. These grocery chains don't want to be places where you can buy groceries for your family; they want to "cause a psychological reaction that makes shoppers hungry." They want to "excite the eye" and "tempt the shopper" into buying more products and spending more money. The science further details the placement of goods within the store's general layout and why (emphasis mine).

"Grocery stores stock the items shoppers buy most often at the back of the store, *forcing* them to travel through other tempting aisles to pick up other essentials. Items such as meat, eggs, diary, and bread are strategically placed at the back of the store, making it hard for shoppers to *resist* grabbing other items when making a quick trip to the grocery store.[15]"

---

[15] I don't know about you, but seeing the words force and resist in regards to grocery shopping is incredibly unsettling.

And it goes deeper[16]. On a further micro level of the aisle's construction, the study explains where and why items are placed specifically on each shelf.

Top Shelf: Local, gourmet, and smaller brands are placed on the top shelf.

Middle Shelf: Middle shelf space is considered the bull's-eye zone, the location that falls perfectly in the shopper's line of sight. This shelf stocks the leading brands and best sellers. Some groceries will sell their prime stocking location to manufacturers for a fee[17].

Bottom Shelf: Store brands and other generic brands are located on the bottom shelf, the shelf that is out of eyesight. Grocery managers know that savvy

---

16 Some grocery stores, especially in dense metropolises where space and storage are limited, employ different techniques to keep shoppers engaged and motivated to purchase. The grocery chain Trader Joe's has a location in Manhattan that employs what can only be described as a serpentine shopping system, whereby customers enter the store, oftentimes after waiting in line outside the building, and get directly into another line that tangles and twist through the store, oftentimes intersecting itself, and the customer is expected to shop, hoping the line slithers to the aisles in which their desired products are located until they can finally reach the cashier. I can't speak to the psychological effects of this because psychologically, I can't bring myself to do that, and I can't really understand how so many people in New York City are, not only capable of doing it but actually make the choice to do it. The assumption is that Trader Joe's has magnificent Bakery, Produce, and Floral sections located in close proximity to the entryway.

17 This is also one of the main criticisms of independent producers of things such as craft beer, where the distribution efforts are not only generally more costly and less effective than those of nationwide or worldwide brands, but they must also compete on a limited shelf space in which the major brands dominate, forcing the craft breweries to compete against themselves rather than with the larger brands who are capable of affording the zoning fee's instituted by some grocery stores.

shoppers will search for a deal[18], so there is no need to waste prominent shelf space on these products[19].

This science is applied to nearly everything in the store, which creates one giant manipulation machine designed to get you to spend more money. And unfortunately, the psychology of shelving is not just restricted to the adult consumer. It has been widely confirmed that one of the most profitable marketing strategies for grocery stores is the whining of children pleading for an item they wish to possess[20] and if grocery stores didn't cater to, endorse, or encourage this behavior in children to sell more products, it would be—if you'll allow me to put on my business hat for a second—a huge "missed opportunity" for them. In order to minimize "distance from unit," grocery stores employ what is known as a "kid's shelf," which is placement designed specifically for children, *"Grocery store managers understand that children often drive a family's grocery purchase. Kid-friendly products are placed in direct line of sight of children."*

I can't say for certain, but I am quite sure that my local corner store doesn't have this level of sophistication in its store design. In fact, it seems pretty much devoid of any shopping psychology tactics, and I can't really tell if it is a benefit or

---

18 No idea how this applies to stores like Grocery Outlet whose whole M.O. is basically bottom-shelf products.

19 Don't mistake the imagery of the bottom shelf; grocery stores literally bend you over before they give you a good deal.

20 Why do you think they put candy in the checkout aisle?

not[21]. If it did, I probably wouldn't hate the deli counter guy so much, I'd be too busy enjoying my "sensory experience" to notice his villainy. But then again, it wouldn't really be an authentic experience. Or would it? Again, I can't tell, and it's starting to seem like that's the point: you're not supposed to notice. You're not supposed to realize how far you have to walk *just* to grab a carton of milk. You're not supposed to think about *just* adding that one more item to your cart. The not-noticing is what this system is designed to do. And that's just for physical locations. That's for stores that have to cater to thousands of individuals passing through their doors (and bakeries and floral sections) every day. Once we get into the digital world, it's a real smorgasbord of shopping psychology. They can (and do) track everything you do on their site, so of course, they are optimized to induce shopping behavior.

To be fair, websites are a little hand-cuffed with respect to providing a sensory experience like grocery stores can; they can only attract your sense of sight through the screen. But what they lack in smells and sounds, they more than makeup for in visual cues and dark patterns. They've developed their own ways of *forcing* shoppers to "travel through other tempting aisles," and they know how to make it just hard enough to *resist* "grabbing other items when making a quick trip" to their website.

I don't need to go into more detail about it because I'm

---

[21] And why am I looking for a benefit when I'm grabbing paper towels and rice cakes?

not trying to go full tin-foil-hat level paranoid about it, but the truth is, it's something I have to think about. I have to *consciously* think about it because if I don't, then all that money and science is going to work, and it's going to make me do a bunch of shit that I don't want to do. And I don't feel that way when I'm back at my corner store daydreaming about beating up the deli guy.

So, maybe there's more to the corner store than just proximity. Maybe there's a lot more. And I don't think it has anything to do with a "hail fellow well met" friendly-neighbor, support local Americana bootstraps kinda bull shit either. It's about something deeper, something more meaningful, more essential than that. It's about humanity. I go to my corner store because I want to feel human. I go there because that human part of me gets fucked up by being manipulated all the time. The human part of me—when I really sit down and think about it—doesn't care about my shopping history or 2-day shipping. It doesn't want endless options and unlimited choices. It doesn't want to have to navigate floors specifically designed to influence buying behaviors. It doesn't like being forced into a psychological reaction by the wafting smells of a bakery when it's just trying to buy groceries. It doesn't want to be monetized and manipulated. It just wants to buy a gallon of milk.

It's only going to get harder. The science will keep being perfected, and the algorithms will keep being optimized.

It's not here yet, but the day is coming when we won't have to leave our house for anything. Groceries, furniture, work, friendships, all of it will be available to us without getting out of bed. More than that, we won't want to. And we won't think it's weird. We'll be conditioned to believe it's a good thing, that it's progress. That it is the inevitable march forward. Maybe it is. I don't know. But if that's the future, I'm going to spend the remaining time I have plodding those 178 paces to the store around the corner.

GOOD WINTER, PART II

Jesse and I arrive in Port Chester a little after 8 p.m. and follow a rag-tag group of suspected fans on a path from the train station to Capitol Theater. With the same general appeal as other small-town theaters, The Capitol Theater is relatively nondescript, lacking a lot of the grandeur of theaters in larger markets. The only indicator separating it from the other low-level buildings lining downtown Port Chester is a thin, unlit marquee banding over the sidewalk out front. It's an older theater, just missing the 100-year-old mark, and the brick exterior, a fading shade of muted Vegas Gold, hovers precipitously between gorgeous and gross. Even accounting for the gloom of this dreary December night, the theater looks as though it's still a few years away from "peak charm" in terms of small-town attraction.

Jesse and I manage our way through security, and after

I make an incredibly exaggerated look of amazement when Jesse says to the man with the clipboard, 'We're on the list,' we secure a couple of drinks at the bar and settle in stage left about halfway down the floor. All the seating on the lower level has been removed and is now just an open, slightly down-sloped space with people clustered into distinct groups. The vibe is somewhat that of a middle school dance. You get the sense that there are a lot of people here with really high expectations but also an extreme amount of uncertainty about how to handle the feelings chaotically coursing through their bodies.

Looking around, the main floor is wrapped by a single balcony that extends across the entirety of the space, terminating in a few sets of those side stage seats I can never remember the name of. Poking just past the threshold are a few scattered extremities hanging over and between the bars of the balcony, the only indication that we are not alone down here on the floor. The proscenium before us, normally a gilded tapestry of flowers and vines, is covered by tall rectangular screens that took me a few moments to realize weren't an additional set of amps stacked one on top of each other, next to the ones that were already there. On the stage is a woman, maybe in her late 20s, with a short black bob cut and an equally-aged-looking man sitting silently beside her behind a computer. An inquisitive gesture to Jesse revealed that he doesn't know who the duo is, and we mostly chatted politely back and forth while they finished their set. But I can tell there's something stirring within Jesse. On the train ride up to the show, after I had released all my pent-up Grand Central tension, Jesse explained why he was willing to put in the extra effort to see this show.

Jesse's knowledge and love of music were well-known to me before we ventured off to Port Chester. Having dedicated the better part of his 20s to diligently working his way through the marketing department of a music management company, Jesse had created something of a name for himself within certain corners of the industry. We jokingly refer to him as the "Czar of Marketing" in our friend group, and the depths of his devotion to music, especially Indie music, the genre in which he works, had always been an integral personality iceberg about him; the immediately noticeable is but a fraction of its magnitude. As the train stretched its way north, Jesse revealed more of this iceberg through a tale of star-crossed struggles in his attempts to see the band Bon Iver, led by one of his musical idols, Justin Vernon, perform live.

"Ever since the *For Emma, Forever Ago* album was released in 2007," he tells me, "I've been trying to see them live and gotten burned every time." Like so many of us, Jesse had used an album as the soundtrack to a break-up, the talisman to keep us centered in times of duress. And as has happened to many of us, an album—its music, its lyrics, and all the emotions wrapped up therein—became that ethereal tattoo we place upon our souls and carry with us throughout our lives. For eight years, Jesse tried to worship at the musical altar that saved the soul of his broken-hearted youth. Not long after Jesse left his hometown of Kansas City to attend Belmont University in Nashville, Bon Iver arrived in Kansas City for a show. More than once, when Jesse returned home for a visit or a break, Bon Iver played a show back in Nashville. Back and forth across the years, the musical sermon Jesse searched for remained just outside his grasp. And then, they stopped touring. The band went into seclusion in the woods of Wisconsin to focus on creating a new album. Jesse's musical eucharist would have to wait.

As the opening act leaves the stage, Jesse stands next to me, beaming with the yearning of the years he'd lost to bad luck. The interstitial ephemera of black-clad roadies setting up is backdropped by a low, dull hum emanating consistently from the speakers. Assuming the noise is feedback or some other indicator of misalignment, I look to Jesse to check his demeanor, worried *he* might be worried that something was wrong. He isn't, and sensing my naiveté as a reasonably inconsistent concert-goer, he begins his masterclass on live music literacy. "They were tuned up long before we got here," he tells me, "They're preparing you—scene setting." His curriculum makes its way through sound crews and lighting technicians before finally making its way to tour scheduling.

"So, why here?" I ask him, still trying to understand why a musician capable of selling out shows throughout

New York was in Port Chest, of all places. "Well, that's the thing," he responds. "He's playing *here*. Then he's playing the Hammerstein on the 10th, two shows at the Kings, and is finishing up at Musical Hall." It takes a few more minutes for Jesse to further explain what he said since I have no knowledge of any of the places he's just mentioned (they're music venues in—surprise, surprise—New York City). All of it adds up to Bon Iver being very intentional about the venues they plays in and how they performs.

In the moments that follow, as the dull hum drones on, I finally get a good look at what the screens on either side of the stage are projecting: 2ABillion. It looks deceptively a lot like *22, A Million*, which is the name of Bon Iver's new album, but I think that's the point. 2ABillion is a social impact campaign created by Bon Iver dedicated to bringing gender equality to center stage and partnered for this show (and all his other shows in New York) with The New York Women's Foundation. It isn't so much a proclamation as it is a presence that permeates the audience. There is an awareness that this is not just a concert but also an opportunity to make a difference. Slowly, though, the message on the screens is replaced with the cryptic symbolism that enshrouds the cover of the *22, A Million* album.

What these symbols are supposed to represent is unclear, but they do a great job of activating the conspiracy-freak part of my brain. At first glance, the religious themes are quite evident, and the iconography evokes an unsettling intermingling of Egyptian hieroglyphics, Christian theology, and dark arts symbolism. Lambs, crucifixes, and shepherd staffs blend with heron silhouettes, obelisks, and ouroboros. A perversion of da Vinci's Vitruvian Man sits below what looks like a smudged QR code. The numerical symbols, of which there are many, mostly seem to be reinterpretations of Arabic numerals with a vague infusion of Japanese hiragana and, again, Egyptian and religious symbols. When viewed holistically, the part of me that wants to believe there is a "higher purpose" and that someone has discovered that "higher purpose" and has encrypted the answer for how to attain it in esoteric markings and pictograms, spends a good deal of time believing that I'm about to ascend right then and there from the floor of The Capitol Theater. It isn't until some of the less profound images begin to emerge from the shadows—a filtered cigarette, a football jersey, a rake, —that I'm brought back down to reality. This coincides with the band finally emerging from the wings of the stage, and the dull hum pitches ever so slightly for the first time.

Jesse's side glance informs me that I am to be prepared. He leans over to me. "We're about to be standing for the length of a movie," he says. "You ready for that?"

"Not really."

"Well, if I start crying, just let it happen, cool?"

"Word."

    A blast of purple light briefly illuminates the theater as the tribal, static-laced percussion of the first song enraptures the audience. The music Bon Iver creates uses a lot of noise—for lack of a better term—to make entrancingly beautiful melodies and rhythms. Intermittent snippets of random audio tracks and manipulated electronic sounds are all over this album. The ubiquitous use of auto-tune and technology I can't really pinpoint masks the lyrics in an almost mystical ambiguity to create an incredibly profound experience, even if it is, for me, at least, nearly unintelligible.

    My inability to distinguish between a lot of the songs means the concert passed by me at a mesmerizing pace and is only now recollected in snapshots, flickering moments of light scattered across my mind. I remember the beginning when a headphone-clad Justin Vernon basked in the meandering emerald spotlight, stood above a 40-foot screen depicting the mysterious symbols from the album, and looked decidedly like the divine figurehead I think Jesse had been looking for all these years. I remember a saxophone solo, hyper-sensualized as the diffused, golden pinlight zoned in on the sax player to the very right of the stage. I remember the same blinding lights from the opening numbers dim and repositioning themselves to reflect candles upon the stage. I remember silhouetted men.

    None of it really made sense to me at the time, and I am only faintly able to comprehend its complexities now. It was—and I hope I'll be excused for saying it—a journey.

As prosaic and cliche as that word has become to describe a musical experience, it's still a serious word, and I'm using it here seriously. What they did, and what a lot of concerts I've been to *don't* do, was transport me. To where, I'm not really sure. But what I am sure about is that for the length of that concert, the experience wasn't (me) at (place) watching (X) like it had been so many times before. This time, the equation was different. I'm not going to pretend to know the answer, but it was something close to (us) plus (them) connecting toward (Y). All of us there in the theater that night went somewhere together. It calls back to the type of music that Bon Iver creates. The lyrical ambiguity is intentional. You're not meant to connect to the words but to the emotions. Take their song, "715 - CRΣΣKS," for instance. To me, it's the most emotional of the album, and a lot of the emotion stems more from what I *can't* understand than what I can. The lyrics that stand out tell a story of loss and pain and suffering, *"Down along the creek, I remember something…That leaving wasn't easy…Finding both your hands…I know it felt right when I had you in my grasp…Oh, then how we gonna cry…Cause it once might not mean something…I see you…"* That's maybe a third of the lyrics. The rest are manipulated through pitch modulation and audio layering or drowned out in some other way, with the effect emulated by how we feel when we go through loss and pain and suffering in our own lives—we can't always understand what's happening, what's going on, or what it's supposed to mean. It's deep. And it's hard to let yourself feel that way in a crowd, which calls back to the intentionality of Bon Iver as a band. They were playing at Port Chester because that's where these things happen. At a smaller venue, they can connect intimately with people in the audience and create an experience *with* them rather than *for* them. I don't know if Jesse was thinking about this when he decided to pick this venue for his first time to see Bon Iver. I suspect that he did and chose to view it as another excavation of his musical iceberg.

After the concert ended, Jesse and I join the bovine line out to the train. The ride back into New York City is more crowded, but it doesn't matter. We find seats near the front of the train, and Jesse pulls out his headphones and furthers my musical education as the darkness of Port Chester gradually gives way to the lights and life of the city. As the train lumbers on, I think back to the beginning. I started the night dreading I would have to travel all the way to Port Chester for a concert with a musician I didn't even listen to. I had been fixated on the emotional toll, perceived or otherwise, that I would have to endure. But this night was never really about that. It was about showing up for a friend when they needed me. It was about uncovering different aspects of the people I surround myself with and connecting.

I don't know if the concert was the musical salvation Jesse had been seeking all these years. It's a part of the musical iceberg that wasn't, and may never be, excavated. But as the train slows into the Harlem station, I look over to Jesse in the seat next to me. His eyes are closed. The deep tones and electronic melodies emanating from his headphones betray a faint hint of what he is listening to while I think to myself, so far, this is a good winter.

THE HORCRUX OF THE PLAN

Most people don't think Horcruxes exist, but I'm not so sure. When I first learned about them as I was gasping my way through Harry Potter and the Half-Blood Prince, it was the mysteriousness of these magical objects that drew me in. The revelation of, and any knowledge relating to, Horcruxes is dispersed in tantalizing small pieces throughout books six and seven of the Harry Potter series. Arguably, they are some of the most important artifacts in the Harry Potter Universe (HPU), and yet, shockingly, little is known about these enchanted items. We know what they are but not where they came from. We know what they do but not how they are made. We know what destroys them but not how they're destroyed. A rough summation of the method is this: a witch or wizard picks an object, performs a ritual, casts a spell, and through this process, a portion of their soul is transferred into the object. Throughout the entire series, this asymmetrical exchange of importance/information in regard to Horcruxes permeates the characters and drives their actions. But, still, by the end of the series, hard, conclusive facts about Horcruxes never materialize.

We know a Horcrux is an enchanted object a wizard places a piece of their soul into as a safeguard from death. In theory, a witch or wizard ablates a portion of their soul into the Horcrux, so if their body (and the soul that remains within it) is ever killed, maimed, or destroyed, they would be able to return to physical existence by using the piece or pieces of their soul that are encased (and thus, protected) in the magical artifact. The whole series hinges on the fact that the main antagonist, Lord Voldemort, created Horcruxes. Truthfully, they are kind of like his whole raison d'etre—he created his first one when he was just seventeen. Yes, he wants to take over the world and subjugate muggles and all that, but the part of the HPU we experience through the original book series mostly boils down to the hoarding, protecting, and eventual destruction of LV's Horcruxes.

Going by description alone, it's difficult to understand the severity of Horcruxes and why LV using them is such a critical conflict in the story. By definition, they're not much different than a savings account; you stash a little bit of something over here, so when that inevitable rainy day comes, you come back and use it. What is being deposited is radically different from your traditional savings account, sure, but the concept is relatively the same. Still, as the saying goes, the devil is in the details. Unlike normal savings accounts, you can't just walk into a bank with a bit of discretionary income and create a Horcrux. It's much more difficult. What a witch or wizard must do to create a Horcrux—and how that process affects those who do—is what makes these mysterious objects so rare. Creating a Horcrux starts with an action the wizarding world widely considers the worst thing a witch or wizard could do: commit murder.

A more detailed description is listed on the online database, Harry Potter Wiki, a website that collates and compiles vast amounts of information from across the HPU.

> *"To create a Horcrux, a wizard first had to deliberately commit murder. This act, said to be one of supreme evil, would result in the murderer metaphorically damaging their own soul. A wizard who wished to create a Horcrux would then use that damage to their advantage by casting a spell which would rip the damaged portion of the soul and encase it in an object."*

It's important to note this act of supreme evil—deliberately committing murder—is the *start* of creating a Horcrux. It's not the culmination of the process or a possible consequence to consider; it's the very first part of a magical procedure that's so antithetical to the wizarding world's beliefs it's only mentioned twice throughout the entirety of the HPU.

The first is from the author of the series, J.K. Rowling. When asked about the method for creating a Horcrux in an interview for PotterCast, J.K. Rowling began with vague intimations of what the process entails before hinting at its true horror. She says, "I see it as a series of things you would have to do. So you would have to perform a spell. But you would also—I don't know if I want to say it out loud…" She never ends up revealing the entire protocol because, as she states later, it's one of the two things she feels are too horrible for her to go into detail about. The other, she says, is how Peter Pettigrew, the treacherous right-hand man of Lord Voldemort, brought his master back into a rudimentary physical existence after he lost his corporeal form trying to murder the infant, Harry Potter. Of the Pettigrew performance, she goes on to mention her editor nearly vomited when she revealed what is required, so we can fairly assume that creating a Horcrux would elicit a similar reaction from the editor, at minimum.

The second mention of the process' existence comes from a book titled *Secrets of the Darkest Art*, said to be written by Owle Bullock (though that authorship is questionable). The book is a medieval archive of evil magic and appears to be the only known source containing the entire technique of creating a Horcrux. As such, it would be a crucial resource for those searching for information about Horcruxes. And, as crucial resources often are, this book—the only one of its kind in existence—was located in a library. Specifically, the Restricted Section of the Hogwarts Library and was only removed by Albus Dumbledore after he suspected that Tom Riddle (aka LV) had read it because Tom Riddle began questioning teachers about Horcruxes.

Personally, I have a serious issue with the Hogwarts Administration allowing this book to remain accessible, but to play devil's advocate (and to avoid a harrowing book-banning tangent), I can understand why they made the decision. Horcruxes, to most of the wizarding world, aren't a thing. Throughout the entire HPU, only a handful of people are even aware a magical process like this exists: LV, Dumbledore, Professor Slughorn, Harry, Ron, and Hermione. It's fair to assume a few of the headmasters and dark arts teachers throughout Hogwart's history knew about them, and a small subset would have intimate knowledge of how they are made. Perhaps one or two high-level Death Eaters would be aware. There is also the author (and one-time owner of the Elder Wand), Godelot, who wrote a chronicle of dark arts called *Magick Moste Evile*, in which Horcruxes make an appearance, but even then, he only mentions Horcruxes in the sparsest of language, "Of the Horcrux, wickedest of magical inventions, we shall not speak nor give direction—" which hints he knows of them, but not the process itself.

Aside from LV, only one person is confirmed to have

created a Horcrux. The other was an Ancient Greek Dark wizard named Herpo the Foul, whose rap sheet also includes breeding the first Basilisk (a monstrous snake-like creature with gigantic venomous fangs and a gaze that causes instant death) and being one of the earliest known Parselmouths, which is a person who can speak to snakes (no judgement, but a trait very much tired to the dark arts). Due to Herpo's intensive study of the nature of the soul during his lifetime and the fact he is the first wizard known to have created a Horcrux, it's widely believed he devised the whole system himself. And while we can assume at least a smattering of other witches and wizards learned about the technique in the roughly 1,200 years that separate Herpo and Owle, there are no other written accounts.

Aside from a few sparse details, the creation of a Horcrux is shrouded in mystery. But even though we don't know *how* it happens, we do know *what* happens, *"a wizard who wished to create a Horcrux would then use that damage to their advantage by casting a spell which would rip the damaged portion of the soul and encase it in an object."* There is no definitive list of what can be made into a Horcrux, and it isn't clear what all the advantages or disadvantages are in regard to objects used in making a Horcrux, nor is it clear how much the witch or wizard's magical ability plays a role in those advantages or disadvantages. There's the obvious disadvantage of natural death if a witch or wizard chooses to use a living object as their Horcrux, so it seems inanimate objects are preferable to living things. But within the realm of the inanimate, there are radically different effects associated with the objects LV uses as Horcruxes. With some, the Horcrux appears to have the ability to induce visions and hallucinations, manipulate the actions of others through mind control, and physically manifest as an apparition of the soul fragment's originator, i.e. Tom Riddle's diary. With others, like the Slytherin locket, it entrenches the wearer in a world of psychological terror. Regardless, all of the objects LV uses as Horcruxes are extremely important to himself but also to the wizarding world at large: his diary, the Gaunt family ring, the Slytherin locket, the Hufflepuff Cup, the Ravenclaw diadem, and his snake Nagini. Once they are created, the Horcrux—or more specifically—the fragment of soul contained within the Horcrux, retains the identity of its creator at that time. This explains why Tom Riddle was still in his youth when he reappeared from his diary in the second book.

And although Horcruxes contain a piece of the soul of their creator, they are (depending on your belief in the existence of a soul) the opposite of a person. A person's container—their body—could be destroyed without any damage to their soul; the fragment of the soul contained inside a Horcrux, however, was dependent on the container for its existence. If the container was destroyed, the piece of the soul encased within it would also be destroyed. This aspect raises some serious questions about why LV would choose arguably the most famous and important artifacts in magical history as Horcruxes, but that's beside the point.

This is a good time to bring up one of the most contentious metaphysical arguments surrounding Horcruxes and the nature of their reality: is Harry a Horcrux? There is vehement opposition on either side of the argument. The pro-Horcrux platform reasons that because a piece of LV's soul was separated and placed within Harry, it satisfies the main ontological requirement of a Horcrux. On the other side of the argument, the anti-Horcrux contingent objects to the classification on the grounds that since LV didn't intend to create one and didn't follow the necessary steps to fulfill the criteria—intentional murder, cast a spell, perform the ritual, place the soul in receptacle—Harry cannot be classified as a Horcrux. Both sides agree the fragment being removed from LV's soul was unintentional, and regardless of where you would cast your vote, it is believed on both sides of the aisle that the inadvertent removal of a fragment of one's soul is, in fact, possible.

Regardless of the receptacle, though, the effects of this process are well known. We learn through the books and supplemental material that Horcruxes have an incredibly chaotic and twisted effect on their creator. The most readily evident is the instability it introduces to one's soul. There are myriad reasons why this is a bad thing, not the least of which is the irrevocable corruption of the person's moral compass.

Amongst all the other atrocities committed by LV, let us not forget our introduction to the HPU starts with him trying to murder a baby. He's driven to this point because a lifetime of destabilizing his soul rendered him incapable of dismissing a prophecy that claimed a child with the power to defeat him was approaching—this prophecy is the reason LV ends up in Godric's Hollow, the home of the Potter family, and successfully kills James and Lily, and tries, unsuccessfully, to kill the baby Harry. Hence the title, "The Boy Who Lived."

A second consequence of creating a Horcrux involves reconciliation or lack thereof with respect to the person that creates it/them. Since the soul has been separated, each of those soul fragments dies individual deaths, never returning to their original whole. This is the reason we see the discarded, child-like manifestation of LV's soul in the King's Cross station after he (SPOILER ALERT!) kills Harry. That is the fragment that was trapped in Harry during the assassination attempt at Godric's Hollow. It was separated from the "master soul" and is unable to rejoin. It will remain stuck in limbo for all eternity; hence Dumbledore's famous proclamation during that scene, "Something that is beyond our help…"

Thirdly is the dehumanization that occurs in the creator. In the HPU, a magical theoretician named Adalbert Waffling proposes in his first Fundamental Law of Magic, "Tamper with the deepest mysteries—the source of life, the essence of self—only if prepared for consequences of the most extreme and dangerous kind." The creation of a Horcrux is the ultimate form of "tampering with the essence of self" and requires from the creator a "tampering with the essence of self" outside themselves, i.e., murder. Once a person's soul has been split, they are no longer a complete person. The psychological damage manifests in the degradation of any moral or ethical standards. A witch or wizard who was willing to commit murder with a complete soul would only be more likely to do it as the soul is separated further. This final consequence made Voldemort the evil and terrifying "thing" that he was. He was no longer human. Not psychologically, emotionally, or even physically, as shown through his snake-like appearance, these are the ramifications one gambles on with Horcruxes. In an attempt to live on Earth forever, the creator risks eternal lifelessness in the afterlife. An objective only the truly evil would desire to fulfill.

Those are the stakes for someone who wishes to create a Horcrux. You risk the stability of your soul, the reconciliation of your essential self, and your humanity, all in an effort to "live" forever. These are some of the most horrific, dangerous, and inhuman creations imaginable. But what makes them truly terrifying, unfortunately, is that these objects are not isolated to the HPU. Enchanted artifacts capable of great evil are embedded in fiction throughout history. Perhaps the most obvious analogy is the One Ring from J.R.R. Tolkien's Legendarium, which, almost one-to-one, matches the criteria for being a Horcrux. But it gets worse. I'm talking about how the horrors of Horcruxes can be found, outside of fiction, in the interactions of hundreds of millions of people around the world every day. Where? Where, in our reality, can we find something that creates instability in our soul? What is something known to cause anxiety, depression, feelings of anger, and irritability? What is something that promotes isolation and prevents us from being present in our own lives? Where, in our real world, is there something where we section off pieces of our soul? Where is there an equivalent to the lack of reconciliation, a place where if we lose all the information from that separate piece of ourselves, it's gone forever? Where have we seen the worst of humanity exposed? Where has the separation of our souls and the stipping of our identity fueled a rise in dehumanizing actions? All of us know where these things happen. What I am talking about, of course, is social media.

This new form of media through apps and platforms in places like Facebook, Instagram, Twitter, Snapchat, and many others—are the real-world Horcruxes I am talking about. These are the receptacles in which we deliberately place pieces of our soul into something outside ourselves. Is the objective the same? Maybe not for all users, but through the multitude of pictures, videos, and memories we post, we can theoretically live on forever. Some say it may be for purposes other than immortality, but I wouldn't be so quick to dismiss that idea.

Besides, whether we use these things for that purpose or not is nearly irrelevant. Through these social media platforms, we *will* live on forever—whether we like it or not. Everything we post will be able to be recalled, in one way or another, for reasons known and unknown and by people known and unknown, seemingly until the end of time. All those little pieces of our souls we have placed on it will survive long after we are gone. In that sense, we have better protection charms than Voldemort did over his own Horcruxes. All that's needed to ensure our Horcrux's survival is the continuous running of web servers.

In Harry Potter, the progression of creating a Horcrux is deemed to be too horrific to mention, but in the real world, it's much simpler. We relinquish some of the most basic and rudimentary parts of our soul—our age, gender, first and last name, and, of course, our email or phone number—and then we complete the excruciatingly ubiquitous incantation *Suscipe verba mea haec et conditionibus* (Latin for: "I accept these terms and conditions"). And then our Horcrux is created. We are now free to place as much or as little of our souls into the corresponding receptacle as we wish.

Thankfully, no person is actually murdered when you sign up for social media but something is definitely killed in the process. As the negative effects on our mental health from social media are beginning to be revealed, any number of users can readily tell you about the parts of themselves that died from social media use, namely their attention and their privacy. We are born with the idea that our privacy and our personal lives can only be ours. While it is true that there are certain restrictions you can place on accounts to protect your privacy and that you are under no obligation to post/interact/use these platforms once you create an account, and yet how many of us have a story about having a conversation with our friends about a topic and suddenly finding a product related to the topic in our Instagram feed the next time we log in? And that's not even mentioning the thousands of data points gathered about our viewing, shopping, and consumption habits that are recorded by these platforms.

These platforms do not start off as evil creations, but once they are imbued with the fragments of our soul, the "essence of our self," they begin to take on evil characteristics. When we have given over so much personal information, willingly or not, to something outside ourselves, its ability to emotionally manipulate becomes its defining feature. Like a Horcrux, these platforms gradually feed on a person's life and negative emotions to strengthen themselves and increase the amount of time users spend using their services. The goal is to show us exactly what it thinks will make us react, and the easiest way to do that is by inundating us with negative feelings. There has been an alarming number of situations in which social media platforms have been indicted for creating what are known as "echo chambers" or intensifying the spread of the villainous "fake news." Like Harry, when he is wearing the Horcrux made out of the Slytherin locket, our irritability and anger increase as we interact with these platforms. Everything we consider our defining qualities, our "essence of self"—our jobs, our hobbies, our relationships, even deaths—are on these platforms and can now be used to trigger us into reacting.

That's not even talking about the dehumanization we endure when we are engulfed in a world entirely crafted from curated moments that create hyper-surreal standards of life. Moments that often are not only physically disingenuous—with all of the reposing, retaking, and editing—but also drenched in emotional insincerity. We're creating visions of our lives that we ourselves cannot even live up to anymore. Whether you feel the pull to document your life constantly or not, it's a good bet that someone in your life does. And just like Ron and Hermione when Harry was wearing the locket, we are crushed beneath the Horcrux's horrible heel just the same.

Perhaps what is most dehumanizing of all is these accounts on these platforms are not "us." A fact so obvious it's ignored completely. Even when you are tweeting, posting, or watching a video of something or someone on a social media platform, you are not directly engaging with a human person even though, like Ginny's obsession with Tom Riddle's diary, these objects are trying incredibly hard to make you forget that. If you post something on someone's wall or retweet what another person has tweeted, that is not an interpersonal transaction. It may seem that way—these platforms do an incredible job of making you feel like they are—but a striking difference exists between a social media interaction and an actual human experience. This, as we have seen, is one of the causes of the rise of cyberbullying and trolling, in which a person's inhibitions to say something—most often negatively—to someone else are greatly diminished because the constructs and consequences of the real world no longer apply. Through this, we become less human, which leads to further breakdowns in the real world. It has become quite common to see groups of people sitting in a room with loved ones or friends, and they are sitting completely silent, staring into the great void of a tablet or smartphone.

The real world even holds space for the contentious "Is Harry a Horcrux" debate in that nearly all of us are creating inadvertent Horcruxes all the time. I found one of my inadvertent Horcruxes recently. I was doing research for another essay when, out of the corner of my eye, something caught my attention. A blink-like disturbance at the bottom of the page, nearly imperceptible, distracted me just enough from what I was doing to call attention to itself. I scrolled down to center it on the screen, and there it was, exactly like I had seen it the last time: A Canon EOS Rebel T3 DSLR camera from Best Buy. It wasn't immediately clear to me I had happened upon an inadvertent Horcrux, but the longer I looked, the little ad began to change. It was not the image itself that changed, but it definitely morphed into something much more than a simple retargeting ad. I stared at the image for a good two minutes until it finally dawned on me that what I was looking at was not a picture of a camera or an ad from Best Buy. What I was looking at was me. It was not me as I was at that moment. But there, buried in the pixels of that screen, was me from six months earlier.

You see, Adam Taft Lambert of October 2016 was BIG into photography. I spent hours researching cameras, film, angles, exposure, aperture, ISO, makes, models, and designs; I completed four or five separate courses on Lynda.com in preparation for the moment that I would get my DSLR camera and tear up New York City. I scoured page after page of information about where to get the best camera in NYC. I didn't end up buying the camera but that didn't matter. There I was, that little piece of me, that fragment of my soul from months ago; the ad retained the identity of its creator when I inadvertently created a Horcrux. Just like LV, I hadn't intended to place a piece of my soul out there in the universe when I was looking for a camera, but it happened just the same. It separated itself from me—me as I was at that moment—and created a Horcrux without my knowledge. These websites and platforms use cookies and caches and whatever else to steal our identities and, in effect, create Horcruxes for us. It's the reason ads for things you look at, talk about near your phone, or mention in a tweet follow you around the internet. Ads for TV shows pop up on your Instagram feed after you talk about Netflix with your friends, or a dress that was considered for purchase is now on the side of your News Feed, and even that camera, that one you never really wanted to buy, showed up months later as an ad on an irrelevant website because of the accidental Horcrux. We have the choice of creating the real Horcruxes, as awful as that idea may seem, but at least we have a choice. We choose to sign up for the account. We choose how much we post. There's debate about how much we "choose" to interact with these platforms versus how much we're "conditioned" to. But, still, with these others, we do not choose. We end up just like LV, totally oblivious to the fact that a piece of our soul has been taken from us.

    If one were inclined, I'm sure the history of social media could be traced back to a single source or origin like Herpo the Foul is for the Horcrux, but what would be the point? Pandora's box has been opened, and we don't have the ability to return everything that's escaped since. Besides, we still wouldn't have the whole truth even if we traced the history because key information for both Horcruxes and social media will continue to be withheld by their creators; we're as likely to learn about the process that almost made an editor vomit as we are to learn about the algorithms directing our social lives. But let's say for a second we did have all the information about social media and Horcruxes we needed; what would we do? Each of us has our choice in the matter. We alone can decide how we wish to proceed. Personally, I'm taking my cue from the very same inciting incident that caused all the Harry Potter drama in the first place: the prophecy that led Lord Voldemort to the home of James and Lily Potter all those years ago. In that prophecy, there is a line—arguably the most important line in the entire HPU—with a premise so powerful it affects the fate of the entire wizarding world. It proposes a solution for how we should regard the billions of Horcruxes we have created and warns us what will happen if we don't:

EITHER MUST DIE AT THE HAND OF THE OTHER FOR NEITHER CAN LIVE WHILE THE OTHER SURVIVES

CONVERSATIONS WITH MY BROTHER #3

On voicemail,

My brother: "Call your mother, asshole."

FIN.

ACKNOWLEDGEMENTS

As you might imagine, there are a lot of people I need to thank who helped make the book possible. My family, of course, gets top billing. They are the perfect blend of stress and support that has shaped me into who I am today. I can't thank them enough for being who they are.

The second is Erin Stover, who has been incredibly helpful in making this dream a reality. Over the months-long process of bringing this together, on the days and nights I would disappear into this project, Erin was always there if I needed her for support, encouragement, and unconditional love. Her editorial eye has been indispensable for this and has once again proved herself the perfect partner. Thank you, my babe.

Finally is my friend Richard Hurley, whose unabashed optimism and unshakeable belief in action spurred this project. Without his constant check-ins, schedule updates, and project management, all of these pages would still be sitting uselessly on computers and cell phones as they had been for years instead of being bound together with hope as they are now.

REISSUE ACKNOWLEDGEMENT

I want to thank Lindsey Amick, who, in addition to being a wonderful wife, mesmerizing mother, devoted daughter, supportive sister, fierce, *fierce* friend, and honorable Hufflepuff, also decided to take on the role of editor for the reissue of this book. More than anyone else, the book is because of her. I pulled this book from the shelves soon after I originally published it because—even though I was proud of what I had accomplished—it wasn't good enough in its original form. It was incomplete, unpolished. Because of Lindsey's keen editorial guidance, grammatical expertise, and compassionate care, these essays are now in a state I am proud of and happy to share with the world. Any errors contained herein belong to me; any credit of excellence belongs to her. Thank you, Lindz. Can't wait to do it again.

WORKS BY ADAM TAFT LAMBERT

HIGHLIGHTS FROM THE FIRST
Collected Essays

ABLATIONS
Poems: Music: Lyrics: Notes

LIMINAL ENNUI
Essays & Stories
(coming soon)

www.ingramcontent.com/pod-product-compliance
Lightning Source LLC
Chambersburg PA
CBHW022108090426
42743CB00008B/769